Bean There, Done That!

by Martin Bean

D1565951

Everything I've learned
about selling IT training.

THOMSON
COURSE TECHNOLOGY

Asia (excluding Japan)
Thomson Learning
5 Shenton Way #01-01
UIC Building
Singapore 068808

Japan
Thomson Learning
Nihonjisyo Brooks Bldg 3-F
1-4-1 Kudankita, Chiyoda-Ku
Tokyo 102-0073 Japan

Australia/New Zealand
Nelson/Thomson Learning
102 Dodds Street
South Melbourne, Victoria 3205
Australia

Latin America
Thomson Learning
Seneca, 53
Colonia Polanco
11560 Mexico D.F. Mexico

South Africa
Thomson Learning
15 Brookwood Street
P.O. Box 1722
Soverset West 7120
South Africa

Canada
Nelson/Thomson Learning
1120 Birchmount Road
Scarborough, Ontario
Canada M1K 5G4

UK/Europe/Middle East
Thomson Learning
Berkshire House
168-173 High Holborn
London, WC1V 7AA United Kingdom

Spain
Thomson Learning
Calle Magallanes, 25
28015-MADRID
ESPANA

ISBN 0-619-16191-4

1 2 3 4 5 6 7 8 9 10   BC   06 05 04 03 02

Table of Contents

Foreword

This book gathers together many of my experiences as well as the lessons I've learned throughout my career in the IT learning industry. In that time, I've seen many changes — changes in technology, in the methods by which training is delivered, and in the way we sell our products and services. One thing, however, has always stayed the same. That is the vital role played by sales professionals in ensuring that our industry maintains both the skill and the integrity it needs to flourish. It is for you, the IT training sales professional, that this book was written.

I've designed this book around *MoneyMaker 2*, a video-based sales training program. I had the pleasure of helping create that program together with a group of talented professionals in the IT learning industry, courtesy of CompTIA, the Computing Technology Industry Association. CompTIA is a not-for-profit trade association made up of more than 10,000 corporate members in 78 countries and 10,500 individual professional IT members from the computing and communications market. With its finger on the pulse of the IT marketplace, CompTIA realized that today's IT sales professionals needed a customized program that addressed the specific challenges of this dynamic market. The result is a six-part training series that tackles a variety of issues on selling in the climate of today's IT industry. The *MoneyMaker 2* program can be purchased directly from CompTIA by visiting either www.beantrain.com or www.comptia.org.

I've also designed this book to be easy-to-read and practical for "hands-on" salespeople. If you're familiar with the *MoneyMaker* program, you'll see that this book is structured along the lines of the MoneyMaker sales model. Many chapters conclude with crisp summaries of my key selling strategies that I've dubbed Beanisms.

Because this project is the synthesis of thoughts and ideas generated by many people, there are many to whom I owe a debt of gratitude. I extend my thanks to CompTIA and to the other *MoneyMaker 2* sponsors for supporting such a worthwhile and much-needed project. Thank you also to all the participants on the MoneyMaker panel. Your insight, sense of humor, and dedication to our industry are appreciated more than you will ever know.

Thank you also to Bonni Frazee, Joe Page, Chuck Lennon, Chuck Wilson, and Gem Skinner. Your ability to transform the thoughts and ideas of many diverse individuals into practical tools that will be used by thousands is a gift.

Last, but certainly not least, my sincerest gratitude to my family. Without the love and support you provide, none of this would be possible. You give me the strength and the energy to thrive in this crazy business we call IT learning.

Now to the book. I hope you enjoy reading it. But more importantly, I hope you will use it to help you succeed and prosper in this exciting and ever-changing industry.

Take care,

Martin

Chapter 1

Introduction

What makes a great salesperson? Is it charismatic charm? A winning smile? A healthy ego? Sometimes it seems there are as many ideas about what it takes to be successful at selling as there are salespeople, especially in the complex world of information technology and IT training. If you've been fortunate enough to enjoy success in your career, you've probably already asked yourself questions like these. And chances are, your experiences have shaped your answers...as they have mine.

For those of us who sell educational services for information technology, our challenges are compounded by the dynamic playing field on which we compete. The rules are constantly changing. We are frequently challenged to think through unusual problems in unique and creative ways. We have to be flexible and ready to respond as circumstances change for our customers or for the technology we're teaching. Our ability to go with the flow, to think on our feet, becomes an invaluable trait when our customers confront us with issues, challenges, or objections that may have never occurred before.

Skills for Successful Selling in the IT Industry

One of the great debates among salespeople has always been the old question of nature vs. nurture — are great salespeople born or made? Well, I've come to the conclusion that a bit of both is needed. An individual with innate selling skills may be a "diamond in the rough," but if those skills aren't identified, developed, and nurtured, that diamond will probably never shine.

You'll soon have an opportunity to study and practice the techniques of a proven selling model as you make your way through this book. But for now, let's consider some of the background skills that will allow you to apply that model effectively with your customers. Take a moment to think about the skills and strengths you can leverage into a track record of success as an IT training salesperson. Ask yourself — is your diamond sparkling yet?

Interpersonal Skills

You've probably heard the saying, "Find a job you love, and you'll never have to work a day in your life." The simple message of that aphorism is that it's a lot more satisfying to be paid for something you enjoy doing than to struggle with a job that's difficult or distasteful for you. This is especially true for those of us in sales. Consultative selling is a career track founded on interpersonal relationships. It follows logically, then, that if you enjoy meeting and interacting with new people, you'll probably have a much better time in sales than an independent soul who prefers working in contemplative isolation. Such people can make a go of a sales career, of course, but the cards are stacked against them if they try forcing themselves into a profession that doesn't suit their temperament.

Salespeople who genuinely enjoy interpersonal relationships sometimes have a natural gift for winning the trust of their customers and closing the sale. You can almost see their enthusiasm in the sparkle of the eyes as they work with customers. Their inquisitive minds draw energy from the symbiotic give-and-take of these interactions, and then convert that energy into sparks of creativity that grow into solutions for their customers.

This attitude isn't something that can be learned or "faked." It isn't a mask that a salesperson puts on in the morning and takes off at night. Either it's there or it isn't. Only you can know how well you enjoy the time you spend with your prospects and customers. Do you wake up in the morning eager to make those first calls to find out what's happening in the lives of your customers? If so, great! Because ultimately, those relationships are what form the basis of trust and confidence that real professional selling is all about.

Communication Skills

Most everyone agrees that the ability to communicate effectively is fundamental to success in all aspects of modern business, and especially in sales. But as I learned on the debating platforms of my elementary school, there's a lot more to the art of effective communication than simply arranging lots of words in clever order. Communication is a dynamic process of listening, thinking, and analyzing information that continues between individuals until a clear understanding is reached. We tend to take this process for granted since "communication" is something we do every day. But as experienced salespeople know, there's a lot more to communication than the simple, day-to-day banter that makes up most of our typical interactions.

Effective communicators are nimble. They can think quickly on their feet, processing information in the background while at the same time communicating effectively in the foreground. This kind of mental

3

multitasking makes it possible for the salesperson to speak in coherent and logical phrases to move the sales process forward while the brain is processing information, planning what will happen one or two steps down the road. Ultimately, these tracks come together as the salesperson and the customer arrive at an agreement on how best to address that customer's real needs.

Diagnostic/Consultative Skills

Consultative selling assumes the ability to diagnose customer needs and provide professional solutions to those needs — solutions that customers could not develop on their own. It is this special knowledge and skill that distinguishes consultants from commodity salespeople. It is also the way that the best consultants/salespeople maintain the interest, enthusiasm, and trust of their customers.

I've always felt that if I'm already working with a customer, it does me no harm to offer a little "free" consulting along the way. I try to leave the door open for other ideas and options, and let my customers walk away from our meetings with three or four new ideas for improving their business. With my broad base of contacts in the IT industry, it's quite easy for me to weave my experiences with others into our conversation. At that point I'm then no longer a salesperson, but rather a broker of information, saying things like, "I was with a customer the other day who had a problem a lot like yours, and you know what he did...?" Or I may call a customer to say something like, "I've been thinking about your situation, and I've got a few harebrained ideas for you — I wonder if I can come out and visit with you to talk about them?"

By the very nature of our profession, we meet and talk with many different people from many different backgrounds. We have a greater opportunity than most in the IT industry to compare ideas, sort the good from the bad, and offer workable suggestions based on our knowledge and experience. Our unique perspective on this industry makes it possible for us to deliver real value to our customers — but only if we recognize those assets, and are willing to go the extra mile to share them with our customers.

Internalized Motivation

Effective salespeople are self-starters. They are confident people who can generate all the energy and enthusiasm they need to do their jobs effectively day after day. They are never crushed by rejection. Of course, rejection is a natural part of the sales landscape, and every salesperson knows what it feels like. Still, there are some people in this business who link their self-esteem directly to their success in sales. Their level of personal happiness or satisfaction is tied to the numbers they see at the bottom of their monthly sales report. This is a mistake that can lead not only to professional failure, but also to personal despair.

The truth is, if we sales types were to internalize all the negative feedback we hear, we'd run the risk of being shattered on a daily basis. Of course, no one likes rejection or criticism. It's natural to respond negatively to it. The problem for us as salespeople is that we simply can't afford the luxury of feeling badly when things don't turn out the way we'd like. If we give in to those feelings, our anger and cynicism will become a self-fulfilling prophecy of negativism that will put us into a death spiral toward personal and professional failure.

It takes discipline to maintain a positive attitude in the face of rejection, but it's certainly not an impossible challenge. You needn't live in a fantasy world of artificial positivism to keep yourself motivated and energized. However, my experience has taught me that there are two things you do need:

- The first is a basic confidence in yourself, and in the products or services you sell. When you know you do your job well, and you are certain that the products and service you're offering are everything you claim they are, then you're ready to sell with integrity and self-assurance.

- The second requirement is a person or persons who can serve as your trusted pipeline to the truth — a way for you to level your perspective with opinions you trust and respect. This might be a spouse, a parent, or a friend. Whoever it is for you, it should be someone you can trust for an honest opinion, no matter what…someone who will always give you the straight scoop,

5

who will help you evaluate your success or failure, and make your plans accordingly.

Commitment

Sometimes, being a success at sales comes down to how much you're willing to give of yourself in order to keep your promises and demonstrate your dedication to the people you serve. Our sincerest attempts to fulfill our commitments may sometimes take strange or even silly turns, but I've found over the years that customers rarely fail to recognize the dedicated commitment of a consultative salesperson, even in the most peculiar circumstances.

Being a salesperson sometimes means just being human, and being honest about it. I remember a day some years ago when I was running late for an important sales call with a prospective corporate client. As I hurried on foot through the congested Sydney downtown, rehearsing my presentation in my head, I took no notice of the darkening skies and the gusts of wind blowing all around me. Suddenly, the skies opened up in a torrential cloudburst. In my rush to get to this meeting, I'd left my office with neither a raincoat nor an umbrella. I tried to protect myself from the downpour with the pathetic remnants of my newspaper, but it did little good. I was soon soaked to the skin.

As I was ushered into my client's office, I felt silly and out of place. There I was, looking something like a drowned rat, dripping onto the deep pile carpet and hoping I wouldn't create any water stains on the elegant mahogany furniture.

My client gave me a wan smile and gestured toward the chair across from her desk. "Thank you for coming, Martin." She said. "I'm so sorry you were caught by the storm. Please, have a seat. I'll be with you in a moment."

I hesitated, but finally settled uncomfortably into the chair across from her desk. I continued to drip.

After a moment my prospect reappeared with a thick towel in her hands. "Here you are, Martin. Please make yourself as comfortable as possible!" I accepted the towel gratefully. As I dried myself, my client said, "You know, under the circumstances, I'd have understood if you'd been late or rescheduled your appointment. I don't expect superhuman feats from my vendors."

"Nothing superhuman at all," I explained. "I made a promise to you that I'd be here, and so I am. Sorry about the carpet," I added with a slight grin.

As silly as I must have looked that day, this customer ultimately closed on a large, multi-year contract that made a critical difference both for me and for my company's bottom line. Yes, I had met her needs, offered value, and provided the services I'd promised, but that wasn't what finally won the day. This client later told me that what convinced her to do business with my firm was the respect I showed her by living up to my commitment to meet with her on that rainy afternoon. I had arrived on time, and was ready to do business — and I'd gone through a lot to do it. She had empathized with my situation. She understood the short-term discomfort and embarrassment I'd experienced, and respected my willing-ness to subordinate my feelings to the commitment I'd made to her. I wasn't about to say, "I can't" to this woman simply because I'd been dampened by a little rain. Our relationship began on a solid footing of trust and mutual respect. We were off to a great start.

So, how about you? Are you ready to begin?

This book has been written to share with you some of the ideas and principles I've learned in my years as an educator, salesman, manager, and strategist in the dynamic worlds of training and information technology. The principles of selling described here are based on the *MoneyMaker 2* selling program, a proven approach designed specifically for those of us who sell into the IT training marketplace. After you read this book, I hope you'll keep it handy as a helper, a guide, a motivator, and a reference tool. As you'll see, some of my core ideas are summarized as "Beanisms" at the end of each chapter. They are there, ready for you, any time you're looking for a fresh idea or some quick inspiration before a sales call!

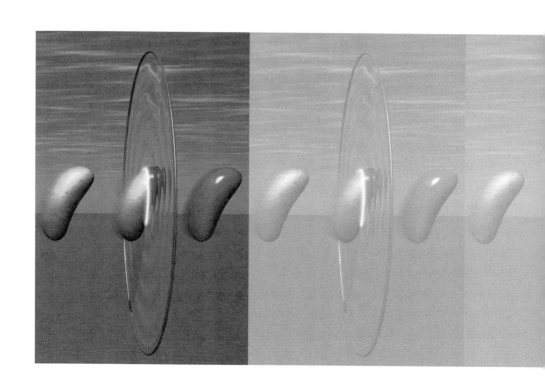

Chapter 2

The Morphing Marketplace: Selling in the IT World

Let's start with the basics. What do you do for a living? You sell. And what do you sell? Education. More specifically, you offer learning opportunities to those who want to develop the skills they need to use today's information technology systems. The fundamental driver that fuels the IT learning business is change…constant change that propels the ongoing transformations in how we work, play, and stay in touch with one another. We know it will never stop. In fact, it will probably never even slow down. If anything, the pace of change will quicken, demanding ever-increasing flexibility from us and from those we teach.

The information revolution has been with us now for over thirty years. In that time, it's become conventional wisdom to assume that keeping up with technology is a requirement for success, not to mention personal and professional empowerment. But as many of us have learned, keeping up hasn't been easy.

Different forms of "techno-anxiety" can be sensed everywhere. We've all heard tired jokes about how the clock on someone's VCR still flashes "12:00," or how they dread the day when the kids go off to college because only they know how to fix the PC when it acts up. In the IT industry, some technical Web sites feature "blooper" pages that poke fun at costly mistakes made by some poor souls who didn't quite understand the technology they were handling. But behind this sardonic humor lies a very real, though seldom discussed, fear: What will happen to me if I can't keep up?

When you think about the dizzying pace of change in recent years, this anxiety seems not altogether unreasonable. Consider, for example, computer users who only a few years ago upgraded from computers that measured data storage capacity in megabytes to systems that handle multiple gigabytes. These same users now face another quantum leap into terabytes, or one thousand gigabytes. After that come the petabytes — weighing in at just over one thousand terabytes each. As exhilarating as the seemingly limitless potential of this new technology may be, we can be forgiven if we have difficulty wrapping our minds around the idea of a single unit of measure, the petabyte, that is equivalent to the storage capacity of about two million audio CDs.

As technology leaps through these exponential changes, the business world is changing right along with it. E-commerce has exploded many old market barriers in recent years. E-business will soon reach the trillion-dollar level in the U.S. alone. As the global IT grid expands, entrepreneurs are developing new business models that focus specifically on customers and their needs. These systems abandon the hierarchical management systems of the past, replacing them with more flexible and adaptive integrated solutions.

Wherever we look, advances in technology and the uses of technology are creating the background noise of modern business. It is this ongoing and omnipresent change that motivates many of the individuals and corporations who come to your learning organization. Whatever their motives may be, virtually all who come to centers like yours have seen the handwriting on the wall, and recognize the advantages that IT education can offer them.

As we scan the horizon for trends in the ongoing IT revolution, we begin to see the form of our future, and what our customers will expect of us. While nothing can be predicted with absolute certainty, several trends have been identified and are beginning to take shape both in the U.S. and across the world. These include:

- Computers will continue to become faster, cheaper, more powerful, and more widely available.

- Bandwidth will increase. This will mean greater use of video and other rich content for distance learning applications.

- Improved data search capabilities will allow learners to more easily retrieve information from vast database libraries.

- Miniaturized sensor technology will improve and applications will expand in many areas, including health care, security systems, industrial quality control, and "smart houses."

- Speech recognition for text and data entry and language translation will become commonplace.

- Security technology that protects systems from computer security breaches will evolve and improve through the wider deployment of firewalls, access control, digital IDs, encryption, and more.

- Wireless technology will be integrated into many network systems where hardwired configurations now dominate. System users who now think of Internet and network access as a desktop-only function will soon go mobile — "online" without the line. Always-connected, on-the-go network access will become commonplace.

Understanding Today's — and Tomorrow's — Information Technology Marketplace

Those of us who teach information technology work in the eye of this storm. We have to work harder than ever to stay at least one step ahead of the curve. We must become "lifetime learners" if we hope to avoid being bypassed both by technology and by our more highly motivated competitors.

Like our customers, we are looking for a coherent picture amid this swirl of change. Unlike our customers, however, we have an added challenge. We have to sort through all the factors that impact not only what we teach, but also how we teach it.

Some of the issues now facing the IT learning industry include:

- *Increased demand for training services coupled with diminishing learner time available for training.*

  The amount of systems knowledge required for corporate employees is increasing. Simultaneously, the amount of job-related time that employees are able to commit for training is decreasing, thus increasing demand for e-learning and blended learning solutions.

  Expanded technology and strong market demand for flexibility are also driving the increased application of technology-driven learning options. Many customers today seek, and often demand, a mix of learning modes that new technology now makes possible. Classroom-based instructor-led training, lectures, laboratory sessions, self-study, interactive synchronous e-learning, asynchronous e-learning, CD-ROMs, and more can now be woven together into a customized tapestry of instruction designed for each learner.

- *The introduction of computerized Learning Management Systems (LMSs).*

  Learning Management Systems help trainers and human resource managers use automation to deliver and administer e-learning programs. An LMS can maximize the efficiency of a learning organization by automating many organizational and record-keeping tasks. It can store and deliver content; administer and score quizzes, tests, and learning exercises; track student records; and communicate with students and teachers. Some LMSs also provide competency instruments and authoring tools to help curriculum designers and instructors provide learning targeted to specific learner needs. These revolutionary e-learning tools typically are scalable and easily modified or updated, allowing even small learning centers to leverage their capabilities to serve larger markets.

- *The expanding role of certification, especially vendor-neutral certification.*

  The IT certification industry has evolved into a widely accepted system for standardizing skills assessment of IT professionals. Individuals seek certifications to enhance their marketability. Corporations look to these programs to enhance their prestige and ensure the skills of those they hire to operate and maintain their technological infrastructure. "Traditional" certification programs such as MCSE (Microsoft Certified Systems Engineer) or Novell's CNE (Certified Novell Engineer™) are now being joined in the market by vendor-neutral programs such as CompTIA's A+®, Server+™, and Security+™, which cross vendor boundaries. Function-specific certifications, such as CompTIA's Certified Technical Trainer (CTT+™) and IT Project+™, are being introduced, and others will soon be added to the mix. Individual learners and corporations can now get the best of both worlds — credentials that assure quality performance standards along with the flexibility to move beyond any single vendor's proprietary solution.

Your Role: IT Learning Consultant

Within this dynamic marketplace, effective salespeople have become more than just conduits for products or services. Today's successful IT learning salesperson is mindful of the confusion experienced by many prospective learners when it comes to deciding what learning path to follow, what technology to pursue, what course options to select, what learning modality to choose, and so much more. Whether they say it or not, many prospective learners want and expect guidance from people like you. They look to you for expert advice. They look to you hoping you'll be willing and able to guide them through the confusing wilderness of choices and options facing them.

Put simply, the customers who contact your center want to speak with a consultant, not a salesperson. They're seeking a professional relationship aimed at solving specific and vitally important problems. They are not coming to you for a cookie-cutter, one-size-fits-all product that you haul out of the back room.

When you become a consultant and not just a salesperson, everything changes.

Your customers are no longer just buying programs and workshops. Instead, they are investing in solutions to real career challenges. You become a resource for personal and professional development. They begin to think of training costs as investments in future growth and development, not as expenses. Most importantly, their relationship with you and your learning organization begins to forge a bond of trust that wins mindshare — that is, the natural tendency of a customer to turn to you and your center whenever IT learning solutions are needed. These ongoing relationships will help you and your center build an annuity of dependable clients who will provide a hedge against economic slowdowns, and build up a healthy learner base to support and build your center's business.

The MoneyMaker Selling Model

There are really no secrets about how to become a successful consultant in IT learning. The first requirement is to simply be there to help your customers when they need you. As important as your presence is, there's a lot more to this than just showing up. In today's increasingly complex marketplace, you must be ready to bring your IT knowledge and experience, as well as program offerings, to your customers. You are challenged to make the connections between their needs and your offerings that will allow your customers to achieve tangible results. In addition, you need to find cost-effective ways to do this so you remain competitive and also earn a healthy profit.

Doing this well can be a formidable task. None of us is born with the skills needed to succeed in this profession. That's why the best way to approach the challenges is with a plan — a plan that allows you to work purposefully and systematically. The MoneyMaker Selling Model is a proven blueprint for just such a plan. This outline has been designed specifically to meet the needs of salespeople like you as you face the ever-changing IT learning marketplace.

The MoneyMaker Selling Model was developed out of the combined experiences of many successful IT salespeople who use a consultative customer-focused approach to sell IT learning. This model is a four-stage process that assumes a focus on customer solutions, not on products or services.

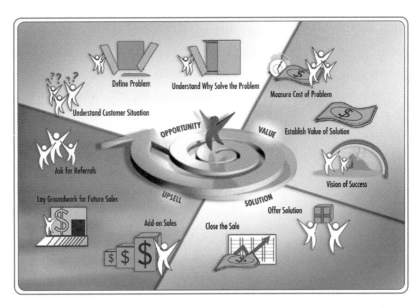

The four stages of the MoneyMaker consultative sales model are:

- Discovering Opportunities
- Establishing the Value of the Solution

15

- Offering the Solution
- Upselling

Seems simple, right? And stated this way, it is. But this basic four-step process incorporates all the key elements needed to develop a customer-focused sale targeted directly at identifying needs and developing solutions to the customer's business problems. As we'll soon see, the MoneyMaker model offers rich opportunities when it's applied and implemented properly. As you might expect, every step in the MoneyMaker model is important, and each of the stages must be implemented in its proper sequence. If you skip a step, you might miss an important customer need and the training opportunity that need represents. You could also fail to build value convincingly. Or, you might miss an excellent opportunity to close the deal or take advantage of add-on sales and referrals.

The time required to move through this four-step selling process, like most everything in customer-focused, consultative selling, is defined by the customer's situation. With one customer, you may be able to work through all four stages of the model in a single conversation. For another, you may need to address each step, or even portions of a step, over a series of sales calls. The amount of time you need for this process may vary significantly from one customer to the next.

We'll examine a variety of practical applications for the MoneyMaker Selling Model throughout this book. Now, let's look briefly at each stage of the model to see how it can work logically and elegantly as a consultative selling tool for IT learning professionals.

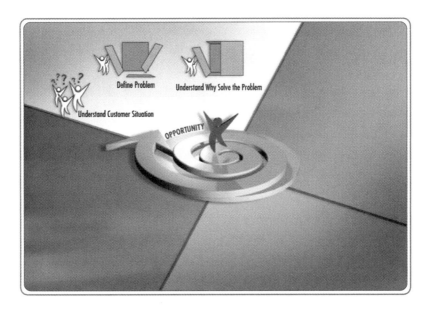

Stage 1: Discovering Opportunities

Stage 1 of the MoneyMaker Selling Model lays the groundwork for the sale by answering three critical questions:

1. Does this prospective customer need training or certification?

2. What is the customer's specific business problem that is caused by a lack of training, or that could be solved with training?

3. Why is it important for the customer to solve this problem? (What will happen if the problem is left unresolved?)

Understand the Customer's Situation

Why is this customer talking to you in the first place? Your first goal is to identify and understand the specific problem or problems the customer is trying to solve with training. You can help yourself focus on this issue by asking questions like:

- What does the customer want that he or she doesn't have now?

- What is the current "pain" this customer is trying to relieve? (Or: What is the possible future "pain" he or she is trying to prevent?)

When your customer tells you about business problems caused by a lack of training, you're well on your way to defining how you can help solve the problem.

You discover and analyze your customer's needs by asking questions and listening carefully to the responses. The questions you ask should start a dynamic conversation between you and the customer. Ideally, you will both open up and discuss a range of needs, strategies, and options that will lead you to the best possible recommendation. The key to your success is to listen carefully to every answer your customer gives you. Then, form your responses based on the information you receive. Let the customer's comments guide the direction of your conversation. Avoid the temptation to follow a mental checklist of prepared questions. If you do, your customer may think you're not listening to what he or she is really saying, and you might miss opportunities to process and incorporate valuable information that the prospect is sharing.

Define the Business Problem

At the earliest stages of your contact, you are prospecting for information. Your goal is to educate yourself so you can define and understand the customer's problem. To do this, start with broad, open-ended questions aimed at giving you a general understanding of the customer's business issues and situation. For example, with an individual seeking training for personal advancement, you might ask questions like:

- What are your current job responsibilities?

- What information technology experience do you have now? (What systems/networks/software do you use in your job?)

- What are your long-range professional goals?

- What has prompted you to think of developing your IT skills now?

When meeting with a corporate representative discussing training needs for a department within the organization, your questions might include:

- What are the strategic goals of this department for the year?
- What types of systems/networks are you running?
- Who are the decision-makers in your organization for an undertaking like this?

Once you have a fix on the customer's big picture, you're ready to sharpen your focus. Your questions can become more targeted as you define the customer's specific business issues that you and your center can solve. These are the problems caused by a specific technical skills deficiency that could be overcome by training. Your challenge is to define the problem — the area where the customer has concerns, feels dissatisfaction, or experiences pain — and then build a solution that addresses that problem. Some examples of questions that can help gather this kind of information include:

- What challenges are this department, or your organization, now facing?
- What kind of customer service problems have you been experiencing with your current system?
- Where are you now having the most trouble with managing your network?
- What led you to think about training as an option? (Have your employees requested training?)
- What steps, if any, have you already taken to deal with these issues? How did they work out?

Describe Why the Problem Should be Solved

At this point, you've defined the problem and drawn a connection between the problem and a training solution. So far, so good. To lay the foundation for the next step in the MoneyMaker selling process, you should help your customer fully understand why the problem should be solved. Your purpose here is to make the customer more fully aware of the pain he or she will feel if the problem is not resolved. Do this by re-stating some of the customer's earlier comments in your own words. You can also ask specific open-ended questions that probe for additional information and help build this kind of awareness. Examples include:

- Where do you think you (your department, your company) will be a year from now if things stay the way they are now?
- What do you think will happen if this problem isn't solved?

A WORD ABOUT RESEARCH FOR STAGE 1: DISCOVERING OPPORTUNITIES: You already know that your time is valuable. Well, your customers feel exactly the same way about their time. The more effectively you manage your time, and that of your customers, the better off you'll both be. In fact, using your customers' time efficiently is one more example of applying a customer-focused selling approach. You can help yourself and your customers save valuable time by avoiding questions that don't specifically focus on your customers' problem or need.

CONSIDER: When you ask a corporate prospect about his or her business, you are looking for background information that benefits you, but not your customer. Questions like, "What does your company do?" or "How many employees do you have?" may give you facts you need to make a sale, but it does nothing for the person you're supposed to be helping. From his or her point of view, this information is old news, and has little or nothing to do with his or her current problems. Research that information before you call on the customer. Your customer will be far more interested if you spend your time ferreting out information on the issues that concern him or her — achieving business goals, increasing productivity, reducing turnover, or whatever else may be causing real pain for the customer.

THE LESSON HERE IS SIMPLE: Do your homework first! The Internet is the most obvious resource for basic research on your corporate customers and their business environments. Other resources include trade journals, newspapers, annual reports, publications of professional associations, and more. Take advantage of these readily available resources to inform yourself before you contact the customers. Pre-call research can give you two important advantages with your prospects. First, it shows your prospects that you care enough about their business to be knowledgeable about it. Second, it allows you to focus most of your interview on the issues and concerns that matter most to your customers.

A WORD OF CAUTION HERE ABOUT STAGE 1 OF THE SELLING MODEL: Some salespeople think that this first stage in the MoneyMaker Selling Model is so obvious, so intuitive, so self-evident that they can rush through it as quickly as possible. Not a good idea! Experienced salespeople know from experience that this step is not as intuitive as it seems. Your customers may not understand their needs accurately or completely. They certainly shouldn't be expected to understand everything you and your learning organization can offer them.

To put it bluntly, the world of IT training is no place for order-takers. Our customers deserve more from us than a pamphlet of course descriptions and a sign-up sheet. As a customer-focused training consultant, it's your job to accurately diagnose your customers' needs, and then formulate the best possible solution you can provide to meet those needs. That will require both knowledge and proactive effort on your part!

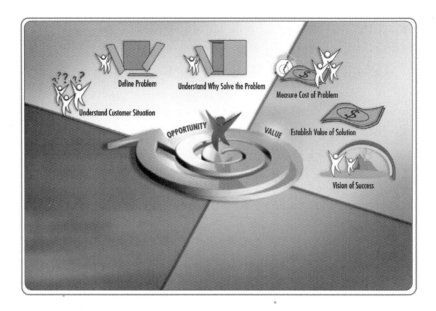

Stage 2: Establishing the Value

The purpose of Stage 2 in the MoneyMaker Selling Model, Establishing the Value, is to prepare the way for offering a solution. In Stage 1, you defined the problem and established a level of urgency by asking the customer to think about what might happen if the situation were not resolved. You are now ready to help your customer quantify the actual cost of the problem, and visualize the benefits of resolving it. Establishing the value is where you paint two contrasting pictures for the customer and set them side by side. The first picture is a nuts-and-bolts, real-world assessment of the situation as it is, or as it will be, without training. The second picture is a "vision of success." This is a detailed visualization of how things will be when training is completed and the problem is solved.

Stage 2, Establishing the Value, has three steps. They are:

1. Measure the Cost of the Problem,

2. Establish the Value of the Solution, and

3. Create a Vision of Success.

Measure the Cost of the Problem

This is where you ask the customer to think about the cost of doing nothing. In Stage 1, Discovering Opportunities, you asked the customer to consider the impact of the problem if things continue as they now are. Here, your task is to quantify the costs of the customer's problem, and assign a value to each cost.

Measures of need vary as widely as the individuals and businesses your learning center serves. Whatever criteria the customer uses to describe the problem should become the benchmark you use for quantifying the problem, and for defining the solution you recommend. This lets you take your solution directly to the heart of the customer's needs. It also makes it much easier for you to describe and clearly explain your proposed solution using terms and concepts that your customer will understand and appreciate.

Consider this example: Sarah Warren, a corporate network manager for a large company, tells you that her group has experienced a significant network downtime problem in the past two months. She thinks this may have been caused by recent software upgrades, but isn't certain. You start your efforts to quantify the problem by asking questions like:

- When did you first become aware of this problem?
- What is the average amount of downtime you are experiencing per week? (How much downtime have you experienced since the problem began?)
- Have you noticed any pattern to the downtime? (Days of the week, number of hours per day, etc.)
- How many times has your network been down in the last month?
- How many of your employees are idled by this network downtime?
- How many total hours of business time does this downtime represent?
- What is the average hourly salary of these employees?

Once you gather this kind of information for a fixed time period, you convert the problem into real dollars-and-cents costs by tallying the salaries of everyone involved with the affected system for the downtime period. This results in a figure for lost productivity that becomes a baseline for "the cost of the problem" — or, stated another way, it provides a hard number for starting discussions and analysis on the cost of not resolving the problem.

In answering your questions, Ms. Warren provides you with the following information:

- Her company's network downtime problem began eight weeks ago.

- IT records show that since that time, downtime has averaged 7 hours per week.

- 800 employees are affected by these outages.

- The average salary of these employees is $35 per hour (U.S.).

Calculate the basic cost of the problem as follows:

Avg. salary: $35 per Hr. × 7 Hrs. per Week = $245 per Employee, per Week

$245 × 800 employees = $196,000 in Non-Productive Employee Hrs. per Week

$196,000 × 8 Weeks = **$1,568,000** Total Downtime Cost to Date

This simplified calculation considers only a few of the fixed numbers associated with the customer's problem. It doesn't consider other, less tangible but potentially important factors such as low employee morale or customer dissatisfaction resulting from service problems caused by downtime. It does, however, give you a solid and very impressive baseline figure to communicate how much this problem is costing your customer.

Establish the Value of the Solution

With the cost of the problem measured and defined, you can then provide an equally clear picture of the value of your recommended solution. At this point, you are not merely defining how a problem will be corrected by bringing the customer "back to normal" — you also want to identify any gains your customer may realize in revenue, productivity, employee or customer satisfaction, or whatever other value criteria you and the customer have identified as important. This is where you can bring ROI — Return on Investment — into the picture. ROI is an important value quantification tool that can be used to measure the earning power or profitability of a business.

We'll be looking more closely at how ROI calculations can be used to quantify and firmly establish value for both individual customers and corporations.

Direct vs. Indirect Cost Questions

Reduced to its most basic elements, all value can be expressed as a reduction in the expenditure of a valued commodity, whatever that may be — time, money, human effort, etc. Your success with customers will usually depend on how well you define the value you offer in relationship to the customers' costs. Some questions you ask will be tied directly to customers' cost issues, while others will be more indirect. Consider these examples:

Direct cost-related questions include:

- How many times has your network gone down in the past month?

- How many of your employees are experiencing downtime because they don't understand how to use your new software properly?

- What is your internal cost justification for the new project you're implementing? How did you arrive at this cost justification?

- How did things go for you when you installed your current system? (What worked well? What didn't work well? What would you do differently if you could do it all over again?)

Indirect cost-related questions include:

- What do you think the effect on your customers will be if you don't train your staff?

- What made you decide to go with this technology at this time?
- Are you planning on certifying your employees once you've trained them?
- What kind of reaction have you had from upper management when your systems have gone down?
- What do you think are some of the key factors impacting the productivity of your staff?

Questions that might help you and your customers quantify the value of the solution might include:

- How quickly do you expect your employees to become fully productive with the technology after the new system is installed?
- How did you arrive at your cost justification for this project?
- What kind of opportunities would become available to you if this problem were eliminated?

Create a "Vision of Success"

The "Vision of Success" is a logical extension of the solution you recommend. It is a word-picture, a visualization of the result of your efforts. Its purpose is to help your customers see how the resolution of their problem will make things better in practical and tangible ways. The more concrete you make this vision, the easier it will be for your customers to justify the cost of training as a means to an end, an investment in making things better.

It is your job as a training consultant to be proactive in creating this vision. As much as your customers may want their problem solved, you shouldn't expect them to be able to conjure up a picture of the successful resolution of their problem. It's up to you to paint that picture, and then hold it up for your customers to see and admire.

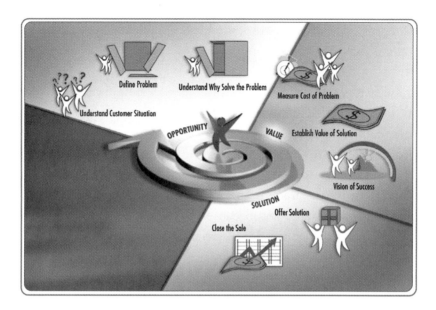

Stage 3: Offering the Solution

In the first two stages of the MoneyMaker process, we've analyzed the customers' situation and diagnosed their problem. For all the back-and-forth we've done, our focus has been on making sure that we've got real needs properly identified, quantified, and set off against the customers' vision of how much better things would be if the problem were resolved.

After this careful assessment is completed, we're ready for Stage 3 — Offering the Solution. The purpose of this critical step is to propose a solution and close the sale. At the same time, you will establish a framework of trust that will lead to a long-lasting relationship. If you've done your job well in Stages 1 and 2, then Stage 3 should come as the natural extension of a consultative, customer-focused selling process.

Of course, you can't depend on something as dynamic and unpredictable as selling to take "natural" or predictable steps. That's why smart salespeople enhance their chances of success by carefully preparing for Stage 3. They craft their proposition carefully and think through all the possible responses their customers may have to the recommendation. Preparation can include preparing backup proposals, developing responses for possible objections, establishing a quantified Return on Investment for the proposal, and having value-adds ready to offer as incentives for closing the sale.

However you present your solution — as a simple verbal recommendation to an individual, a formal written proposal to a corporate committee, or something in between — careful preparation is critical. It is especially critical for those of us in the IT industry, where knowledge of technology, training options, and market trends is often assumed by our customers. The unprepared salesperson in this highly technical and ever-changing business usually fails because — despite the traditions set by Willy Loman and his generation — you cannot succeed in this market "on a smile and a shoeshine." As experienced IT professionals know, today's technical market is very unforgiving. Simply put, you should never try to "fake it" with IT customers. Your technologically sophisticated clients will always be quick to recognize inaccurate or incomplete information. The risks and the cost of failure are much too high.

When proposing your solution to a customer, use trial closings along the way to verify that you are on the right track with the customer. A trial close can take the form of simple and unobtrusive questions such as "Does that sound right to you?" or "Are you with me so far?" Such questions are simple tests that ensure the customer's agreement with any assumptions or recommendations you've put on the table. They allow you to check on your customer's attitude toward your proposal while you're presenting it. They help you uncover any unspoken questions or concerns, and also verify the customer's tacit approval of your offer.

Closing the Sale

All the work you've done up to now leads you to this decisive point in the sales process — closing the sale. This is where the rubber meets the road. Without a close, everything else you've done is pointless. Because it is so important, some salespeople become anxious when the time comes to ask for the sale. Actually, if you've done a thorough job up to this point — identified the customer's problem, examined the options, and defined the best solution — then your close will follow the next logical step in your consultative problem-solving process.

As in every other stage of the MoneyMaker Selling Model, questioning techniques play a key role in closing the sale. Effective closers use direct or indirect closing questions, depending on their reading of their customer's readiness to move ahead. A direct closing question is assumptive. It takes the customer's "yes" for granted by looking ahead to the implementation of the proposal. An indirect closing question is evaluative. It lets the salesperson check for any last-minute objections or concerns before moving ahead.

Examples of direct closing questions include:

- Are you ready to move ahead with this proposal?
- When would you like to schedule the start of the training sessions?
- Can we move ahead with scheduling?
- Can we do business today?

Examples of indirect closing questions include:

- Do you think this solution will solve your problem?
- Does the solution we're proposing fit in with your business needs?
- Do we have an understanding?
- Have we been able to meet all your requirements with this proposal?
- Is this what you're looking for?

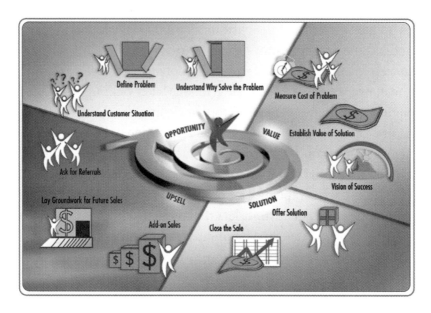

Stage 4: Upselling

The final stage of the MoneyMaker Selling Model is Upselling. The purpose of this step is to establish and develop a relationship with the customer that bridges you from the first sale to the next, and beyond. This is the stage that takes advantage of the groundwork you've already laid by:

- Gaining add-on sales during a current close,
- Re-setting the stage for additional sales cycles with the customer in the future, and
- Asking for referrals.

Upselling should be the easiest type of sale you make. That's because you've already done most of the hard spadework. Your customer is now qualified, needs have been identified, background research has been done, and you've learned through experience what does and doesn't appeal. Despite these obvious advantages, many salespeople fail to take advantage of the upselling opportunities available to them. Why?

There's no simple answer, really. Perhaps it's an innate "love of the hunt" that motivates some salespeople to prefer the challenge of pursuing elusive new prospects to the less exhilarating task of cultivating existing business. Maybe it's a lack of awareness that so much opportunity still exists with these customers. Whatever the reasons, smart salespeople know that when it comes to getting the most "bang for the buck" — the greatest potential income with the least amount of effort — nothing beats upselling.

At the Close: Looking for Immediate and Future Add-On Sales Opportunities

Look for chances to upsell every time you close a sale. While you're preparing your proposal to address a customer's immediate needs, ask yourself if there are other courses or certifications that might be appropriate for this client, either now or in the future. Then mention them after the closing is complete.

Laying the Groundwork for Future Sales

As your relationship with the customer evolves, you have many opportunities to educate the customer about other learning and certification options you provide. When you offer this information, you not only prepare the way for future sales, but also enhance your credibility, your trustworthiness, and your potential future value as a learning resource by reminding your customer that you are there to meet his or her needs — however those needs may develop.

Asking for Referrals

This tried-and-true technique for building business can be used at any time and with virtually any customer with whom you come in contact. A phone conversation, a brief chat before or after a class, a luncheon meeting — all these and more are opportunities to ask for the kind of information that can lead you to a new and successful sales cycle. Asking for referrals is easy. The hard part is simply remembering to do it! Train yourself to never pass up a referral opportunity.

Questions to ask when requesting referrals may include:

- Who else do you know who could use this type of training?

- Are there any other departments in your organization that might benefit from a similar solution to the one we've developed for you?

- Do you have any peers whom you think might benefit from a training solution similar to what we've provided for you?

Beanisms

The Morphing Marketplace — Selling in the IT World

The only constant in the IT world is change

Change is a constant factor affecting both what and how we teach. Change propels constant and ongoing transformation in technology and business. While the hectic pace of this change may seem chaotic, it is a source of limitless opportunities for those who are clever enough to recognize them and nimble enough to take advantage of them.

Selling is about discovery, not manipulation

The stereotype of the used car salesman wearing a loud sports jacket embodies a common prejudice: Salesmanship is a form of manipulation, a way to "trick" people into buying things they don't really need. As all true sales professionals know, this cliché has nothing to do with real salesmanship. Real selling is a shared process of discovery in which the salesperson works with a customer to identify needs, and then matches appropriate goods or services to meet those needs.

Under-promise and over-deliver

Never let your customers down by failing to keep a promise. Don't just meet your customers' expectations — exceed them. When you do more than what you promise, you will pleasantly surprise your customers. You'll also establish yourself as a trustworthy and unexpectedly valuable resource in your customers' eyes. This can prepare fertile ground for future repeat business and upselling opportunities. It also buys you the good will that every salesperson needs when something goes wrong. Remember: While successes are often remembered, failures are never forgotten!

Create a vision of success for your customers

Help your customers "see" what your proposed solutions will do for them. Build a mental picture of what their organization will look like after they invest in your training solution. Ask, "What will happen if you don't address this problem?" Then, demonstrate and quantify the value of your solution.

34

Reach for the "low-hanging fruit": Don't miss upsell opportunities

Remember that upselling a current customer is the easiest sale you can make. You already know a lot about your client's business and probably have ideas about his or her future needs. Avoid the common mistake of thinking too much about closing sales with prospective new accounts while overlooking the rich opportunities you've already uncovered.

Selling IT training is not about taking orders

Successful IT training salespeople are customer-focused training consultants who make it their business to accurately diagnose their customers' needs, and formulate the best possible solution to meet those needs. For salespeople to do well in today's competitive marketplace, they must be able to demonstrate knowledge, invest proactive effort in their customers' interests, and apply that knowledge to help solve their customers' problems and deliver a return on investment.

Use your customer's time efficiently: Focus on needs

Use your time wisely. Complete background research before you meet with your customer. Learn what you can about the customer, the company, the challenges they're facing, and more by doing research on the Internet, or through other resources.

Create a tangible vision of success for your customer

Effective salespeople know how to use a customer's aspirations and hopes to build value. When we create a tangible vision of success for our customers, we rekindle those hopes while also offering a means for helping transform them into a reality.

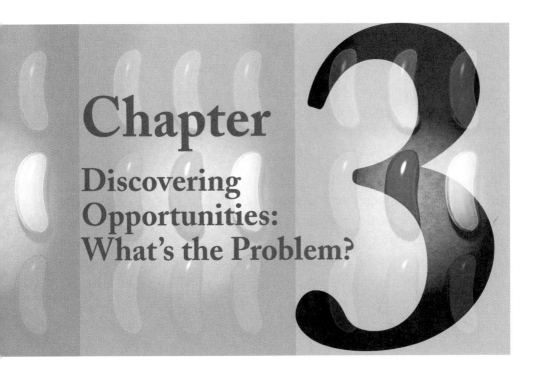

Chapter

Discovering Opportunities: What's the Problem?

In Chapter 2, we saw how the start of the selling process, discovering opportunities, is where we lay the groundwork for every sale. We do this by gathering information about what the customer needs, and processing that information to prescribe the right solution to address those needs.

In this chapter, we'll look more closely at the first stage of the selling model, and see how it answers three fundamental questions that every consultative salesperson must ask. We'll consider some of the key differences between the individual and the corporate customers who buy IT training. We'll also examine ways you can help your customers quantify both the cost of their problems, and the value of your potential solutions.

The three questions at the core of Stage 1, Discovering Opportunities, are vital prerequisites for the rest of the selling process. They are:

- Does the customer really need training or certification?
- If so, what is the customer's career or business problem that training can help solve?
- Does this customer clearly understand why the problem is worth solving?

When you begin Stage 1 with a new customer, you're usually starting at baseline zero. You know little or nothing, and you can't begin to offer value until you gather and process a lot of important information. Since you have so little to work on, you must collect your information quickly and efficiently. This is where communicating effectively with your customers, the core skill for all sales, is most critical.

Gathering information from customers is challenging enough, but as every consultative salesperson knows, this stage is even more complicated than that. To effectively discover the opportunities your customer may present, you must not only ask effective questions, but also think on your feet. You must be able to quickly synthesize and process the information you gather, and present it back to the customer in the form of more focused, redirected questions that will lead you and your customer toward a clear definition of the problem and the best possible solution you can offer.

Selling to Individuals, Selling to Corporations

When we look at the customers who learn with us, we see a tremendous variety of people all bound together by one common goal. They want to develop skills that will allow them to be more effective and successful. Regardless of their professional backgrounds, IT training customers want to become more efficient, more effective, and more valuable in today's technology-driven world. Our customers come from all walks of life, and from every imaginable career category. A typical workshop or lab today may include educators, civil servants, and government employees working alongside corporate managers, graduate students, business administrators, and many, many others.

From your perspective as an IT training salesperson, this bewildering variety becomes much less complex when you focus not on who learns, but rather on who buys. It is the purchasers of training services who ultimately determine your success or failure. These critical decision-makers belong to one of two groups: They are either individual buyers — people seeking to develop their own IT skills — or corporate buyers — representatives of companies looking for external vendors to help their organization develop the skills of their employees. Each of these buyer categories has unique motivations, incentives, and goals. Each also offers its own special advantages and challenges for you and your organization.

Individual buyers are a growing opportunity within the IT training market. These potential customers are motivated, conscientious, and eager to learn. They may be young and inexperienced workers trying to break into the IT industry, or they may be older professionals looking for new opportunities. Regardless of their particular circumstances, these individuals have made the decision to take charge of their lives and proactively steer their careers in a new direction.

That decision takes courage. While these individual learners may be decisive about their decision to change, the wise training salesperson knows that they are probably anxious about what they're doing. Individuals tend to be cautious and tentative when shopping for training services for two very good reasons:

- They're making decisions that could mean significant changes in their lives. Their hopes for a promotion, a new job, a new location, or even a whole new tax bracket may be riding on the choices they make with you.

- They're spending their own money. Individual buyers often have limited budgets and may be unsure whether their investment in training will really pay off. You must be prepared for these value-based concerns whenever they arise. You should also be prepared to discuss creative financing options for individual customers who may need it.

The individual buyer often needs more information about technology, training options, and opportunities in the marketplace than corporate buyers. You'll usually spend more time with these buyers as you provide guidance and direction about their best learning options. Remember that your consultative guidance can be critically important to your individual customers. While they may require extra patience and empathy, it is this kind of one-on-one consultative approach that most truly characterizes customer-based selling.

One important note about this customer segment: When marketing your training services to individual buyers, make sure that you are aware of any state or federal regulations that govern your ability to sell education directly to these customers. At the state level, a number of very specific "do's and don'ts" exist to protect consumers, and these guidelines vary widely from state to state. In fact, some states prohibit training sales to individuals by individually owned and operated IT training companies.

For more information about these guidelines, contact your state Department of Labor or local Better Business Bureau, or check the appropriate links at www.beantrain.com. Be sure that you understand these regulations and how they may affect your business to ensure that you avoid any penalties or refunds to individuals you've trained, or find yourself precluded from selling to that market segment in the future.

Corporate buyers represent organizations that have identified a need for IT training. For corporations, this training is a means to an end. Corporations purchase IT training services in order to:

- Achieve a competitive advantage,
- Improve their ability to accomplish specific business objectives, or
- Solve specific business problems.

For you and your learning organization, an obvious advantage of corporate buyers is the sheer volume of business they can represent. Individual customers buy one program at a time. Corporate buyers may potentially invest in many different programs for large numbers of employees. Clearly, corporate buyers of IT training services are fertile ground for the IT training industry — ground that no successful learning organization will leave untilled.

Both buyer groups are important. The most successful training companies today have discovered that a healthy mix of individual and corporate customers creates a productive atmosphere for learning as well as for success in the business of IT training. Whatever ratio may be right for your center, keep in mind that the market need is real and pressing for both learner categories.

Discovering Opportunities for Individuals

Individuals who visit companies like ours to buy training services almost always ask some form of the question, "What can you offer that will enhance or advance my career in the information technology market?" For many of these individuals, finding ways to finance this training is an important and complicating issue. Individuals are often cost-conscious buyers who will be spending their own money for the services they buy. Indeed, it is often the chronic lack of cash that compels some buyers to seek out IT training in the first place as a path to financial freedom and even wealth.

It amazes me how much confidence some people place in the IT industry as a dependable pathway to personal prosperity. Of course, the definition of prosperity varies from person to person, as I learned a few years ago when my wife and I hired a young contractor to repair the gutters on our home. When I arrived home from the office and pulled into my driveway, I noticed that our young gutter repairman was still working away up on the roof. As I got out of my car I glanced into the front seat of his pick-up and noticed a dog-eared CompTIA A+™ manual lying there amidst his work orders and hardware receipts.

When he finished his work and came down off the roof, I mentioned to my gutter man that I'd noticed his manual and knew a little about IT training and A+ certification myself.

"So, what was it that got you interested in studying A+?" I asked.

Well, you know," he said, "Fixing gutters just isn't all it's cracked up to be. I really want to get off of people's roofs, and start working where you can really make some money...in the computer industry."

A short while later, he handed me his bill. I stood there, in stunned silence, shocked at how much I was being charged to have my gutters repaired. I then thought to myself, "He's got it all wrong. If this fellow really wants to get rich, why would he ever get out of the gutter repair business?"

When asked why they're looking for IT training, many individual customers offer one of these explanations:

- *I want a better job.*

  This is the most common reason given by individuals when asked why they are inquiring about IT training options. These learners make no bones about their goals: They want an opportunity for more responsibility and a higher salary, either with their current employer or at a new company.

- *I want a more meaningful career.*

  For this customer, the primary goal is personal fulfillment. Financial growth takes second or even third place in priority. The value of a career choice for these buyers may be more difficult to quantify because it cannot be measured in strictly financial terms. You'll need to probe carefully and engage in longer discussions with these buyers to form a clear picture of the values driving their decision for change. This is especially true if they haven't yet identified a career path that will give them the satisfaction and value they seek.

- *I want to stay ahead of the curve.*

  These learners want a job that will put them on the cutting edge of technology and keep them there. These buyers may be very knowledgeable and come to you with a clear goal in mind.

Others may have only a vague awareness that they lack the skills they need to get ahead. It's your task to apply careful questioning and listening skills early in your conversation to clarify this customer's background and general learning needs.

- *I want to be "with it" — to do what everyone else is doing.*

  This consumer is following the crowd toward something new and exciting. A hint that you're dealing with this type of learner comes when you hear something like, "I don't know much about computers, but my friends keep telling me that this is where it's at." These learners often talk about their friends or relatives with jobs in IT. They have been convinced by these people that developing technical skills will be their best path to a better, more secure future.

  When you meet these prospects, don't be surprised if they have no firm idea what they want, either in their career or from your training organization. They may not even be able to clearly explain why they're contemplating this step. Selling to these individuals requires patience, understanding, and empathy. It's also common for these customers to be unfamiliar with the language and the culture of IT. In your conversations, be sure to choose your words carefully. Avoid any jargon, industry acronyms, or other terms that could be confusing to the IT novice.

Serving the individual customer can be extremely rewarding. There will be occasions when you'll see the advice you've given transformed into action by customers who use their IT skills to launch a new and exciting chapter in their lives. The Discovering Opportunities phase of selling to individual customers can also be a long and time-consuming process. Because these consumers tend to be warier than their corporate counterparts, they require more intensive one-on-one consultation that includes rapport-building, relationship development, and constant reinforcement.

The anxieties they feel are natural, and your patient empathy with their concerns will be important to them. By listening carefully, asking the right questions, and successfully guiding your customers toward the right choices, you'll help them overcome the fears that stand between them and their goals. When you do that, you'll have offered some of the most valuable services that any customer-focused sales consultant can ever provide.

Understanding the Individual Customer's Situation

Typical IT training customers freely acknowledge that they don't know as much about information technology as they should. Individual buyers may have clear career goals in mind — say, advancing to a management position within a department or organization — but they often have only vague ideas about how to accomplish that goal. When dealing with these customers, you become most valuable when you provide the personal motivation, guidance, and support that enhances the learning programs the customer has come to buy.

Whether your customers approach you with a clear vision of their goals or just a vague feeling that they need IT training, the key to helping them is in the careful application of questioning skills aimed at probing for motivation. The process begins by asking open-ended questions that encourage the customers to speak broadly about their situations, then listening carefully to the responses. Open-ended questions lead customers into discussions about how they came to think of training as an option. This, in turn, can get them talking about their needs and business problems.

Early in your contact with a customer, frame your questions to encourage the customer to explain, to describe, and to offer as much information as possible that will help you qualify needs and solutions. Examples of effective qualifying questions for individual customers include:

- What are you doing now? (Or: Are you currently working in an IT-related field?)
- What's your background or level of experience for your current position?

- What are your long-range career goals?

- What are your specific responsibilities in your current position?

- Do you have personal responsibility for these systems, or do you share responsibility with others?

- What training have you had for the work you do now? (When did you have it? What subjects were taught? How was it taught — classroom? Self-study? Computer-based training? Etc.)

- Have you ever tried learning on a computer or on the Internet?

- How did you feel about the technical training you had before? (Did you like it? Did you think it gave you what you needed to do your job well? If you could go back and do it over, what would you change?)

Defining the Problem for Individual Customers

Often, the qualifying questions you ask will reveal or hint at the situation or problem that led the customer to consider an investment in IT training. If the customer doesn't volunteer information, ask for it directly with open-ended questions like:

- Why are you thinking you want to make a change?

- What caused you to decide to call/visit us today?

While responses to these questions can be as varied as the marketplace, some of the more common answers heard by IT trainers include:

- I was passed over for a promotion because I didn't have skills needed for the new corporate system.

- My job is boring. There's no challenge to it. I get no satisfaction out of what I do.

- I've got too much to do in my job, and not enough time to do it. I get overwhelmed by doing lots of tasks by hand that I know could be handled a lot more efficiently using computer technology.

- I feel like I'm falling behind. My customers are asking me to bring them fresh ideas using the latest technology — and lots of times, I don't know what they're talking about!

- I read about all the money you can make in IT jobs (or computer-related jobs).

If the customer's answers are not as clear or straightforward as these, you may wish to switch to closed questions that prompt more focused responses from the customer. For example:

- Are you looking for increased income?

- Are you hoping to gain a promotion to a more prestigious position in your company?

- Do you want to find a more interesting job than the one you have now?

Building Value: Why Solve the Problem?

Building value in Stage 1 of the selling model can be particularly effective with individual customers because the consequences of this question impact them directly and personally. Motivated individuals who see IT training as the solution to their career needs have already felt the pain of their situation, and won't require much incentive to tell you about it. Your questions in this area will resonate loudly. To help your customers clarify the importance of resolving their problem for themselves, consider asking questions such as:

- What do you think will happen if things continue for you as they are now?

- What will happen if you do nothing?

- What do you think will happen if you don't develop your IT skills?

Your goal at this phase of your selling process is to establish the criteria that will allow you to define the cost of the problem. Once the standards of measurement and the cost of the problem are set, you have what you need to establish the value of your proposed solution, and to describe that value in concrete and persuasive terms.

A word of caution about some individual buyers who may call on your learning organization: They may not be individual buyers! Some corporations will send representatives posing as individual buyers to scout out different training vendors. These "mystery shoppers" will tell you they're interested in personalized training for themselves when, in fact, they are evaluating your facility before sending you an RFP for planned corporate training needs.

Companies will offer two reasons when asked why they engage in this kind of subterfuge. First, they hope to save time and bother by evaluating your operation "on the sly," without involving themselves in the normal vendor solicitation process. As they see it, they'll save time and reduce their exposure to time-consuming follow-up calls if they send their own "Trojan horse" to assess your operations. Second, they believe they'll get a more accurate picture of your organization's operations if they check you out on their own terms. Corporate buyers who've sat through lots of vendor presentations may see value in avoiding all the marketing glitter by checking out your facility from the learner's point of view.

Keep this possibility in mind as you speak with your individual prospects. Don't make the mistake of assuming that your individual customers may not also be interested in how your programs can address typical corporate priorities such as improved productivity, efficiency, and profitability.

Discovering Opportunities for Corporations

Corporations are a significant market opportunity for IT learning organizations like yours in terms of their volume and profit potential. When dealing with prospective corporate customers, keep in mind that the overriding goal of all corporations can be stated very simply: They want to make a profit.

As a professional IT sales consultant, your task with corporate customers is to demonstrate how the services you offer will help corporations achieve their business objectives. You must demonstrate your ability to provide value — either directly or indirectly — to the corporation. The extent to which you succeed at this task will determine your success.

What motivates corporations to consider buying from external vendors? Some key drivers for these decisions are to:

- Achieve an advantage over the competition,

- Improve the ability of the corporation to accomplish its business objectives, and

- Manage or resolve specific business problems.

Discovering opportunities with corporations is inherently complex. Your first challenge is to clearly identify the decision-makers — a problem you don't face when dealing with individuals. Corporate customers also typically require a careful and thorough needs analysis to define their situation and the business problems they face.

As a rule, your corporate customers will be less personally invested in the buying decision and more focused on profitability and efficiency than their individual counterparts. The corporate buyer is generally happiest when you use his or her time as efficiently as possible. What might appeal to an individual buyer as conscientious probing and attention to detail may strike the corporate buyer as an unnecessary waste of time. As we've noted elsewhere, you can earn valuable points with corporate decision-makers by doing background research before you call, to learn about the corporation, its products, its challenges, and its IT training needs.

Identifying the Corporate Decision-Maker: When and Why?

No matter how much time you spend in a corporate setting, little or nothing will actually happen until you interact with the person who has authority to make a buying decision. It is clearly important that you identify that person and get him or her involved in the process as soon as possible. It does you no good to convince a corporate representative that your training programs are right for them only to find out they must pass on your suggestions to someone else who has the final say. You can help yourself avoid this problem with a simple and straightforward question like, "Is there anyone else involved in making this decision?" Or "Who signs the check for programs like these?"

It would be helpful, of course, to find out up-front if the person you're speaking with can make the buying decision, but avoid the temptation to ask this question before you first establish trust and good rapport with your prospect. You don't want to risk offending the customer by sending an early message that your primary focus is on making money. Establish first and foremost that your first goal is to solve problems or provide services for the customer. Once that point is clearly made, you can then move on to identifying the person with decision-making authority.

Understanding the Corporate Customer's Situation

Corporate customers present you with a more formidable challenge than individuals simply because you must gather, process, and analyze so much more basic information. When you speak with corporate customers, ask them to supplement any information you've developed during your pre-call research by asking them questions such as:

- What is your current IT infrastructure?

- What is your current training budget?

- How are your employees currently trained on your existing technology? (How do you now handle IT training in your organization? What kind of training do you now offer? What systems/technology do you teach? What methodology do you use?)

- What system enhancements or changes are now being planned or envisioned? (Software, hardware upgrades, etc.)

- What specific business issues or problems are you now attempting to address with your current training initiatives?

- Is there upper-management support for your current training initiative? (Or: For an expanded training effort?)

- What is your time frame for solving your problem? (Are there "time to market" constraints associated with this issue?)

- Would you be open to an integrated or a blended approach to learning in which we would combine e-learning with classroom instruction to tailor the best possible solution for you?

- What is your decision-making process? Are you the decision-maker? Etc.

Defining the Business Problem for the Corporate Customer

Business problems can almost always defined as a variance, or gap, between a situation that currently exists and a desired goal or objective. Your first step in defining the problem is to identify that target or end goal. If the corporation has clearly defined its objectives, its people will probably also have developed and implemented a plan to achieve them. It is not your responsibility to either agree or disagree with that plan. As a consultative training professional, your task is to use your knowledge and experience to evaluate their strategies objectively, and offer training solutions that will help them more efficiently get where they want to be.

The best way to clarify a problem for corporate customers is to define it in terms of their stated strategic goals. In well-managed organizations, larger goals are reflected within the performance targets and business plans of every department and group within the organization. When you familiarize yourself with the corporation's larger goals — either through pre-call research or questioning — you'll be prepared to evaluate the information you gather against these objectives.

Don't be surprised if you discover some contradictions between the stated goals of an organization and the objectives of a department, division, region, or project team within that organization. It's common for outside consultants to uncover internal contradictions and inconsistencies in large or highly compartmentalized organizations. You may be able to help both yourself and the corporation by pointing out any inconsistencies you, the outside consultant, can see that may be invisible to those working close to them.

A very effective open-ended phrase to use when defining business problems that can be solved by training is, "Help me understand…" This phrase encourages the customer to provide factual information about system infrastructure (types of systems, numbers of servers and nodes, number of system users, key applications, etc.). It can also prompt the customer to provide process information that can illuminate how well the company's IT infrastructure is helping the corporation achieve its goals.

Corporate customers considering IT training are typically faced with one of three basic challenges:

- Newly hired employees must gain skills needed to operate existing technology,

- Current employees must gain skills needed to operate new or soon-to-be-installed technology, or

- Current and future employees must gain skills needed to implement new technology in the future.

Building Value: Why Solve the Corporation's Problem?

When you understand your products and services well, you will be able to evaluate the opportunity presented by your corporate customer with detailed specificity. At this point, you want to create a clear picture of what will happen to the customer if the problem is left unresolved. Consider asking a question like, "What do you think would happen if your untrained employees stay on in their present jobs?"

At this early phase in the sales process, you are preparing the customer for your proposed solution by first creating what amounts to a vision of failure. This vision portrays a hypothetical end point the customer may reach if the corporation fails to take action on its problem.

This vision of failure can also serve you well if the decision-makers in the corporation offer one of the most common objections to training recommendations. When consultants like you offer suggestions for skill development programs, corporate managers often express concerns along the lines of, "What if my employees want more money, or leave us after we've spent money to train and certify them?" Your best response is to turn that question around by recalling the vision of failure. Ask simply, "What if you don't train them and they stay?"

As always with the corporate customer, your questions should be aimed at defining why the problem needs to be solved on the mission-critical or goals-critical issues for the company. Collect this data with questions like:

- What is the current cost of system downtime in your organization? (Use this figure to help calculate ROI.)

- What do you figure as the total cost for the company in dollars per person hour when the network goes down?

- What happens to your sales, service, and profitability when mission-critical systems in your corporation fail?

- What do you think would happen to you if we're not able to solve this problem?

If you are now serving corporate customers, you already know that the complex challenges facing organizations today can rarely be resolved with simple, one-size-fits-all solutions. Standard certification tracks or generic packages that might have worked as a corporate training solution at one time are less and less likely to meet the real needs of today's increasingly sophisticated corporate customers. The careful research and analysis you do during Stage 1 of the MoneyMaker model, Discovering Opportunities, will increasingly steer you and your prospects toward customized and blended learning solutions.

The questions you've asked and the information you've processed in Stage 1, Discovering Opportunities, have helped you lay the groundwork for the next phase of the MoneyMaker Selling Process — Stage 2: Establishing the Value.

Beanisms

Discovering Opportunities – What's the Problem?

All purchasers of IT training belong to one of two groups: Individual buyers & corporate buyers

Individual Buyers are...	Corporate Buyers are...
• Motivated by a desire for a better job or more personal fulfillment from their careers.	• Motivated by a desire to achieve specific business objectives or solve problems.
• Appreciative of your time and attentiveness. They require patience, hand-holding, and personal guidance.	• Appreciative of your efficient use of their time. They require objective data, and evidence of your past success.
• Careful shoppers who are spending their own money.	• Typically operating with a fixed training budget.
• Anxious about wasting their money.	• Anxious about high-visibility failure.
• Responsive to visions of personal success.	• Responsive to ROI calculations backed with statistical evidence.
• Often in need of financial support or guidance to fund their programs.	• Concerned about implementing and measuring transfer of knowledge from learning to the workplace.

If customers are anxious about the cost of training, make them even more anxious by considering the cost of not training

When you recommend a training solution, you may hear concerns along the lines of, "What if I train and certify my employees and they ask me for more money, or leave?" Respond by turning their question around. Ask the customers, "What if you don't train them and they stay?"

Discovering opportunities is a dynamic, "think-on-your-feet" process

You have little or no information at the start of a selling process. As a consultative salesperson, your task is to gather the information you need quickly and efficiently, synthesize that information, and incorporate what you learn into your subsequent questions and comments. This is a dynamic process of give-and-take that can lead you both to the best possible solution you can provide.

Selling IT training to individuals calls for patience, understanding, and empathy

While the sale to an individual may not be as profitable as a corporate account, it can be more rewarding on a human level. These individual sales often take more time and demand more hands-on consultation that includes initial rapport building, relationship development, and reinforcement — but the effort can definitely pay off. The advice and guidance you give your customers may be just the impetus they need to launch a new and exciting chapter in their professional lives. (And who knows? Your successful individual customers may become managers who send you lots of corporate training business in the future!)

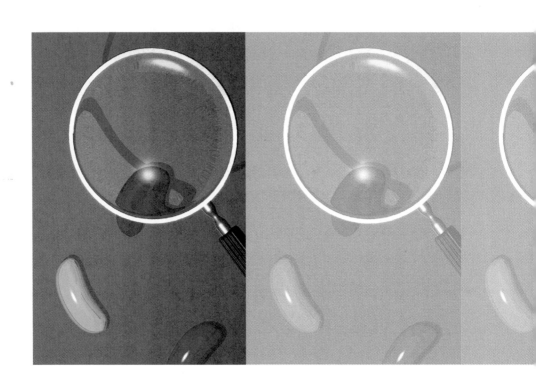

Chapter

Establishing Value: What's the Cost of the Problem?

You've done a great job with Stage 1. You've clarified your customer's IT training needs, and helped him or her understand why he or she should take action. You sense that things are going well. Perhaps you're even thinking ahead to a successful close. In your eagerness, you might be tempted at this point to leap right into offering a solution. But you don't.

Why? Because you're a customer-focused IT consultant and not a commodity vendor who sells products based on price. You know that you are dealing in solutions that can have life-changing impact on individuals and businesses. What you're doing is too important for a cookie-cutter, one-size-fits-all approach. You know that there's still work to do before you and your customer are ready to finalize an agreement. This is why it is critically important for you to carefully apply Stage 2 of the MoneyMaker Model — Establishing the Value of the Solution.

In Stage 2, you will measure the true cost of the customer's problem in quantifiable terms that are important, meaningful, and clear. You'll then use this information to create a vision of success that will counterbalance the vision of failure your customer has already seen. You will help your customer fully appreciate the benefits he or she will realize from the action steps you will soon recommend. By building value here, you are also improving your chances of success by creating a pre-emptive barrier against objections that could arise when you make your offer. Put simply, you are giving your customer a clear and compelling reason to take action.

Your tasks in Stage 2 of the MoneyMaker model are to:

- Measure, in quantifiable terms (time, money, output, etc.), the cost of a customer's problem.

- Establish the value of your potential solution applying the same cost criteria you used to define the problem.

- Create a vision of success that clearly illustrates how your solution to the problem will bring tangible improvements for the customer.

The Value of "Value"

How careful would you be about making a decision that could put your entire future on the line? For your individual customers, that's often how they see the choices they face with you. From their perspective, they are taking a big chance in the hope of building a brighter, more prosperous future. You are a part of a life-changing process that is often highly personal, emotionally charged, and concerned with a lot more than just getting a pay increase.

The cost of your services may be an issue for these customers, but for most, value will mean a lot more than the price you charge, and it will seldom be the only factor influencing their buying decision. Your individual customers may listen to everything you say, but the unspoken question echoing in their minds will be, "Yes, but will this work for me?" If you can show these customers that you really can "make it work," then you will have succeeded in defining value for them — and probably succeeded in clearing the way for a successful sale.

One way to enhance your customers' perception of the value you provide is to apply the principle of "under-promise and over-deliver." This simply means setting realistic expectations with your customers from the very start, and then doing everything you can to exceed those expectations. By doing this, you'll not only validate your training services, but also give your customers that most rare consumer experience — the delight of getting more than they were expecting.

Building Rapport While Establishing Value

Building rapport simply means setting a warm, welcoming tone with customers to create an atmosphere of openness and trust. Establishing good rapport with individual customers can be easy, and will go a long way toward overcoming the natural anxieties these customers often feel. When you offer your customers the kind of personalized attention that makes them feel welcomed and special, they will be much more inclined to trust you and the proposals you'll make.

Experienced IT training consultants know that individual buyers are often influenced toward a buying decision by the level of commitment and enthusiasm that you, the sales consultant, show for your training organization. If you and your fellow employees are sincere and passionate about your organization, it will make an impression on every customer you meet. Never be shy about letting your customers know how proud you are of your programs, your instructors, and your track record of success. Your passion will send a signal to prospective customers that can in turn spark their own passion for the possibilities you offer.

Set a warm, friendly, and relaxed mood during conversations with prospective customers with such simple communication skills as:

- Personalizing the discussion by occasionally using the customer's name.

- Using consistently positive and upbeat language.

- Maintaining a natural, informal, and friendly conversational tone.

- Making use of your sense of humor. (But be careful — don't overdo it!)

Questioning Skills for Establishing Value with Individuals

Your questions during Stage 1 were your initial attempts to collect information. You cast a wide net to gather the facts and figures you needed to define the opportunity and prepare the basic framework for your sale.

Now, you're ready for more targeted questioning. In Stage 2, your questions should guide you toward the specifics you need to quantify and analyze your customer's training needs. With that information, you'll be able to define both the cost of the problem and the gains your customer could realize from a potential solution. The answers you receive to your Stage 2 questions will also prepare you to apply a powerful technique for calculating the earning power of an investment in training and establishing value for your customers — ROI, or Return on Investment.

But first, you need more facts. As we've seen, defining and quantifying a customer's problem consists essentially of identifying what a customer wants and comparing that to what the customer already has. The gap between these two points is the "problem" your customer wants to overcome. Your work in Stage 1 told you that the IT skills or certification training you offer could be the right solution to that problem.

Your task now is to measure the cost of that problem. As in Stage 1, you start with open-ended questions targeted to elicit more detailed descriptions of the customer's situation. For individual customers, you will often use this strategy to review and clarify the problems your customer is now facing. Ask questions like:

- What's making you feel dissatisfied in your job?

- Why do you want to make a change at this time?

- How do you feel about your current salary?

- How do you think your lack of training in these areas is affecting your job performance?

- How are changes in technology affecting the way your company does business? How are they affecting your job?

- What kind of difference do you think certification could make for you?

- Where do you want to see yourself professionally five years from now? What do you think you'll need to do between now and then to make that happen?

As your customer speaks, you will at times want to re-direct the conversation to uncover a specific fact or sharpen your focus on a particular point. To do this, switch to closed questions — questions that can be answered with "yes" or "no," a number, or another one- or two-word response. When these closed questions lead your conversation back in the right direction, follow up with additional open-ended questions that will encourage your customer to clarify and expand on the information you need.

Examples of closed questions that can re-direct a conversation with individual customers, along with some logical open-ended follow-ups, include:

- Are you feeling frustrated with your job? (Why?)

- Have you missed advancement opportunities in your current position? (What happened? Why do you think you missed out? How did this make you feel?)

- Do you think you're making what you're worth? (Why not?)

- What do you think you should be earning? Or: What would you like to be earning? (How do you think learning new IT skills will help you accomplish that salary target?)

- Do you think you're as productive as you should be in your job? (What makes you think that?)

- Do you feel like you're working extra hours for free because you don't have the skills you need to be efficient?

As your customer provides information, verify your understanding of the points he or she makes. Ask confirmation questions and restate key points to make sure you understand the customer correctly. For example:

- So, if I understand it, you like your current job, but you think your growth options are limited because the company's so small. Is that right?

- You said earlier that your objective is to increase your income by at least 20 percent within the next year. Do I have that right?

- Let me make sure I understand… You're basically happy in your present position as a network administrator, but you think you'll have more credibility and growth potential if you earn these certifications. Correct?

What's in It for Me? Establishing Value with Individual Customers

While you can do a lot to build trust with your individual customers, trust alone will not trigger a decision to buy from you. Establishing value with new customers is more than just a matter of reassurance — it's a matter of proof.

Think about it: No matter how positive your first impression of someone, you're naturally wary at first about entering into any commitment that requires trust. That's reasonable enough. After all, you don't know the person. You have no idea what he or she can or cannot do. Perhaps you've even had a bad experience in a similar situation in the past. The customers who call on you to inquire about IT training services come with a built-in wariness that will only be overcome when they become convinced that what you're offering will be right for them, and is worth their investment of time and money.

So, how do you validate the claims you make? How do you create both realistic expectations of value and potential results for your individual customers? Consider trying some of these proven techniques for building trust while establishing value in your learning organization:

- *Share testimonials from former students.*

  Real-life success stories from former students can be compelling demonstrations of the value of your programs and services. Consider asking your successful graduates to write letters that describe how your programs have benefited them. Share their comments with your prospective students as well as your current clients who may be considering additional programs. Don't hesitate to share your past achievements to lay a solid foundation for future success!

- *Share data from independent research studies.*

  Reports and studies prepared by IT industry research and consulting organizations can be found at Web sites such as www.comptia.org, itaa.org, gartner.com, prometric.com, idc.com, vue.com, and others, and offer substantial independent data that can help you validate the advantages of your IT training services. These research studies can also be useful starting points for discussions about the more subjective benefits of IT training, such as greater job satisfaction, increased advancement opportunity, and marketability. (For more information about independent research on the IT market and IT training, visit www.beantrain.com.)

- *Maintain a current list of IT "help wanted" notices.*

  Something as simple as a collection of classified ads from your local papers can help you demonstrate the breadth and depth of career opportunities for today's job hunters who have certified IT skills. These job listings, along with those found on Internet job boards such as monster.com, can be used to initiate discussions about a customer's specific needs and the curriculum choices that may be right for him or her.

- *Invite prospective customers to "career nights" at your learning center.*

  This cost-effective marketing strategy can give prospective customers a chance to see for themselves how learning takes place in your environment. Encourage your prospective individual customers to speak with your students, especially those who will soon graduate. Have them ask your students for their first-hand stories about your programs, as well as their future career plans.

- *Offer "lunch and learn" events.*

  Encourage curious prospects by offering free mini-sessions about common or popular applications during the business lunch hour. Make arrangements to have salespeople and enthusiastic instructors available at the session to answer visitors' questions and describe the value-added benefits of your center and its programs.

  If your company is a provider of only e-learning courseware, think about offering the equivalent of a career night or lunch-and-learn over the Web to provide a great experience for your prospective learners and an excellent marketing opportunity for you.

- *Provide financing options for customers who need it.*

  Does your organization have a program for pre-screening prospective customers for financing? If not, consider starting one. Many successful learning organizations use programs like these to "pre-approve" prospective clients for financing. Some find that they can close a sale with 30 to 40 percent of these prospects simply by addressing concerns about financing early in the process.

  Learning organizations that aren't able to administer their own financing programs sometimes set up relationships with nearby financial institutions to serve their students' needs.

  However you handle it, think through a way to offer financial assistance, either directly or indirectly, to your prospective customers who may need it. This value-added service can be just the incentive an undecided prospect might need to make a buying decision in your favor. As we noted earlier, you should be mindful of state and federal regulations governing the sale of educational services to individual learners to make sure you handle these issues properly.

Clarifying Return on Investment (ROI) for the Individual Learner

Defining Return on Investment for your individual customers is often a more subjective process than the more precise calculations associated with corporate ROI. You obviously cannot guarantee any learner's success, either with your programs or in his or her career. Too many unpredictable variables prevent you from offering hard-and-fast assurances to your learners.

You can, however, demonstrate the potential value of an investment in your programs by:

- Reviewing job and salary profiles for positions now available in your market. (Get out those Sunday classified job listings or visit online job services.)

- Identify and highlight specific positions that require the skills or certification you're discussing with the prospect.

- Review your prospect's current job and earning power. Compare that information with a representative average of salaries and benefits offered by employers currently advertising for skilled IT professionals.

With this kind of information, you can use this simple ROI formula to present your prospect with an impressive hypothetical scenario of potential future potential:

Solution Value (Potential New Annual Salary)

—

Solution Cost (Investment in IT Training/Certification)

=

Return On Investment (Income over Current Potential — 1st Year Only)

This simple, hypothetical ROI calculation can then be refined further to identify a payback point — that is, a date on which the customer's investment will be paid back in full. After that point is passed, all of your customer's increased income goes straight to his or her bottom line.

Your customers are ready to earn more money and have more satisfying careers — but are they ready for the challenges they'll face in your IT training programs? You will serve your customers well if you first verify that they have the skills they need to succeed with your curriculum. Targeted qualifying questions during your interviews can help you assess skill levels and place your learners into appropriate programs that are right for them.

You can also help your customers evaluate their current skills while also providing an impressive "value-added" service by offering free skill assessment tests to your candidates. An assessment will give an objective evaluation of learners' skills that can help them avoid failure and frustration by guiding them to the right programs from the start. It will also make the learning experience more enjoyable for your instructors. They can be confident they have the right people in their classrooms, students who are capable of learning and grasping the material.

Using Certification to Establish Value with Individual Customers

Certification services are a natural tool for establishing value and validating the benefits of your IT training. A certified learner can offer prospective employers evidence that he or she possesses specific skills required for a job. Individual learners are frequently drawn to IT training organizations with the specific goal of passing a particular certification test, or meeting certification requirements for a specific job assignment.

Not all customers are aware of certification as an option, or how it can help them. For customers who might benefit from a certification track, you can provide a valuable consultative service by first explaining the concept. Reinforce the benefits of certification by sharing information about the advantages it offers.

You and your organization can incorporate certification into your marketing efforts in many ways. Techniques that have proven successful for some IT learning companies include:

- *Offering certification test preparation lab nights*

  Consider sponsoring special lab nights dedicated to helping certification candidates improve their chances of passing the test. These events give participants an opportunity to gain hands-on experience with simulated tests. They can also discuss the test with trainers and fellow students, and ask questions about the testing process. These preparation sessions give many learners the added confidence of a "trial run" before they commit themselves to the actual examination.

- *Providing add-on business or placement skills for students*

  You already know that most of your individual customers are learning new skills or are working toward certification to prepare for job changes or career moves. Why not proactively offer value-added services to help them with this process? Resume consultation and preparation, job-interviewing skills, and communication skills are examples of services that would require little effort on your part, but could provide a valuable boost for your anxious job candidates. In the long run, as your graduates make plans to address their future training needs, these services can become an investment in their ongoing loyalty to you and your organization.

- *Developing apprentice programs to give newly certified individual students experience with your corporate clients*

  Build synergy between the individual and corporate sides of your business by encouraging mutually beneficial apprenticeships for certified learners. These arrangements are often "win-win" opportunities for everyone: Students gain valuable hands-on experience in a corporate environment. Corporate employers gain skilled workers at comparatively low costs, and can extend offers for full-time employment to apprentices who prove themselves. Your training company gains gratitude and respect by solving yet another "problem" for your customers!

Certification can be a valuable resource for building value with individual customers, but it should not be your central focus. Remember that certification is a means of assessing IT skills — it does nothing in itself to teach or build those skills. The hard work of certification is in the skills development that comes beforehand — the training. This is why focusing only on certification or the certification exam can be a risky marketing technique for IT salespeople.

Consider, for example, individuals who shortcut their way into the IT job market by "cramming" for the certification test. While they might pass after several attempts, what real value will they bring to an employer who hires them based on that certification? Other students may struggle to achieve a particular certification, win a challenging job based on that certification, and then discover too late that they're beyond their depth in a position too challenging for their overall capabilities. More failure, more frustration.

The bottom line: When using certification to establish value with your customers, sell carefully!

Defining the Value of the Solution

Perhaps your customers have been blocked from the jobs they wanted. Perhaps they've taken a recent salary cut, and now see it as a cost of not being certified in a particular system or skill. Whatever the problem, you've put the pieces in place to show your customers the real value of solving the problem.

If you're prepared with the right facts and figures, this becomes a simple matter of looking at the solution from the perspective of the customer's problem. For example, you could describe the types of jobs that a person with a particular certification can obtain. You may also mention the current salary ranges and benefits packages that these positions offer. Cite examples of former students from your center who have taken the path you're recommending and obtained the types of jobs or promotions your customer wants. Remember to mingle together your quantifiable financial benefits with those appealing to personal growth, satisfaction, and fulfillment. You can build your value statements around a mixture of tangible and non-tangible benefits such as:

- Higher salary and improved financial security.
- More free time.
- Improved personal and career satisfaction, credibility, and self-esteem.
- Ability to perform the same job tasks in less time.
- Potential for salary increase, etc.

Building Value: Creating a Vision of Success for Individual Customers

Your next task is to continue building value by assembling a coherent picture of what this value will mean for your customer. You can do this as a question that encourages your customer to picture the benefits you describe as realistic and attainable possibilities. For example: "How would you like the increased prestige and opportunities that would come from knowing how to…?" Or, you might tell a "real world" success story that creates a vision of success based on the issues the customer has already defined as important. For example, "I remember a student we had last year who had a job like yours. He got his A+ certification from us, and he went on to…."

If your customer has already heard success stories about other students you've trained, use them to draw parallels with the potential benefits your customer may realize. Underscore the validity of this "vision" for your customer by revisiting the objective statistical resources you described earlier. These may include salary surveys, ROI studies, and industry reports. Use data from these resources to objectively validate the possibility that the vision of success you describe can, in fact, become a reality. Involve your customer as you weave this tale of success by asking him or her how he or she wants and expects the story to turn out. Remember that you're not spinning a fantasy — you are giving substantive shape to your customer's own stated aspirations and goals.

If you've done a good job capturing information and verifying its accuracy along the way, then this image should strike your customer as something surprisingly clear, vivid, and achievable. With this picture in your customer's mind, you are now ready to set before him or her the specific solution you have in mind that's just right for him or her.

What's in It for Our Bottom Line? Establishing Value with Corporations

Whatever stands between a corporation and its ability to achieve its profit goals is, by definition, a problem for the company. Your corporate customers will almost always appraise their relationships with you and other service providers in terms of your ability to demonstrate, in clear and quantifiable terms, how you can help them overcome problems that impact their bottom line. The more successfully you establish value in these terms, the more successful you will be with this important segment of your market.

Your corporate customers will expect you to provide facts and figures to make your case. But remember that all corporations define value in their own way, and your description of the value you can provide should coincide with their definition of just what the term "value" means.

What are the corporation's priorities? What are its stated goals? Where does the company see itself five years from now? If you did your job in Stage 1, you should already have the answer to these and similar questions. As you've seen, the key to successfully establishing your value for corporate customers is to tie your proposals to the value criteria spelled out in the corporate customer's business plan, or the corporation's defined business needs. Once you've identified the value criteria that are important for the corporation, you are ready to build your case by calculating value in terms of your potential Return on Investment for the customer.

Prioritizing IT Training — Short-Term Costs vs. Long-Term Value

If corporate customers define value as bottom-line profitability, where does IT training fit into the profit picture? For many companies, IT training becomes an issue only after a major capital investment has been made in new computer hardware or software. As managers become aware of the need for training, there is often little left in the budget to deal with it. Decision-makers in such situations will often define short-term value as "making do" until the next budget cycle comes around.

In such circumstances, your challenge is to help your corporate customers understand the real costs the company will ultimately pay if its system operators are not given the skills needed to use their systems as efficiently and effectively as possible. It isn't easy to overcome short-term expediency thinking, especially when budgets are tight and technical training is considered an expendable luxury. If you have the facts and figures to demonstrate that your corporate customers will reap long-term benefits from an investment in training, then you have a responsibility to present your case as clearly and persuasively as you can. When you succeed, you'll have created a real "win-win" scenario for everyone.

You can use a variety of approaches to establish the value of IT training solutions for your corporate customers, including:

- *Form an action team that includes both IT Managers and the IT Training Manager.*

   As an external IT training consultant, you will often encounter corporate IT managers who are reluctant to work together with department or group managers who have their own IT responsibilities. You can overcome this problem by casting yourself in the role of an external intermediary committed to addressing company-wide IT issues.

By forming a cross-functional action team, you can define yourself as a coordinator, not a problem-solver. Your role is to consolidate the challenges facing the organization and to help the team develop solutions to the problems shared by different groups within the organization. Make it clear to everyone that recommendations made by this interdepartmental team of IT specialists will be much more likely to receive upper-management support than suggestions received from a single interest group within the organization.

- *Prepare to demonstrate — not just describe — how your solution will solve the customer's problem.*

Clarify the issues and concerns that seem important to the decision-maker or decision-makers. Develop costs based on as much hard data as you can obtain from the customer. Associate those costs directly with these important issues so you can build a solution that links directly back to the stated goals and objectives of the company. As you build a solution, be prepared to use this hard data to develop simulations or scenarios that will illustrate how your solution will perform in the customer's real-world settings.

- *Stay up-to-date: Check for any changes in conditions as your sales effort progresses.*

Corporate sales are often negotiated over time. They may require several calls on decision-makers and others to gather the necessary facts for your proposal. As your corporate selling process moves forward, be sure to check for any changes in the customer's situation that may have occurred along the way. When changes occur, be prepared to think on your feet by modifying your plan to accommodate those changes. Keep in mind that the IT system and training needs of dynamic corporations are constantly evolving. You will enhance your value as an IT consultant to these customers if you can react quickly and positively to the changes you encounter.

ROI and Corporate Customers

Return on Investment, like the idea of value itself, is a concept that varies from customer to customer. This is another reason why it is so important for you to figure out exactly how your customers measure value. Your customers may even refer to this technique for quantifying value by different names. Some corporate customers may call it RONA (Return on Net Assets). Others will tell you that they calculate ROCE (Return on Capital Employed). Still others may develop their own unique criteria for quantifying and measuring value. Whatever terminology they use, all of these techniques are variations on calculating Return on Investment, and all are intended to quantify the value of an investment made to solve a problem or improve profits.

As we've seen, the basic formula for calculating the ROI you can provide is:

Solution Value – Solution Cost = ROI

If you successfully completed Stage 1 of the MoneyMaker selling process, you defined the customer's problem and established how the customer defines the cost of that problem. As you now set about to calculate the Return on Investment for your customer, you will incorporate that data into this calculation. Typical values developed for this kind of calculation may include costs for:

- System downtime.
- Lost employee productivity.
- Increased service time per customer, resulting in lower total volume.
- Poor service delivery.
- Low morale, resulting in increased employee turnover.

The Solution Value for your ROI calculation will be the benefit realized by correcting or improving that situation to the level desired by the customer.

The Solution Cost is the corporation's investment in the IT training services you offer.

The Return on Investment is the difference between the Solution Cost and Solution Value that will result from the services you provide.

Validating Your ROI Strategy

Before calculating a specific ROI for your customer, build confidence and trust in your programs by reviewing industry-specific case studies that describe the experience — and the ROI — of similar companies. Corporate customers generally respond well to objective evidence about trends in their market and the experiences of companies similar to theirs.

Case studies can provide an excellent starting point for "what if?" discussions with your prospects. You can use these cases to explore the issues facing your customer within the context of how those issues have already been handled by others. As you describe the hard numbers reflecting the experiences of other corporations, you can freely explore various options and consider their ramifications for your prospect's company.

Testimonials can also be effective tools for confirming your credibility with corporate clients. Something as simple as a short letter on corporate letterhead from a satisfied customer can go a long way toward building confidence in your ability to deliver the results you promise. Don't hesitate to ask corporate customers who have benefited from your services to give you such a written testimonial. Ask them to include as many specifics as possible about the programs, the instructors, and the beneficial results of doing business with you and your organization.

Some of your satisfied customers may be willing to provide references for you and your company. Consider asking these satisfied clients if you could provide their names and phone numbers to potential customers as a referral for your customers who face similar training challenges. Few marketing tools are as powerful as the enthusiastic affirmation of your organization by a customer who has benefited directly from your services.

Creating a Vision of Success for Your Corporate Customer

An ROI calculation goes a long way toward building a clear picture of the outcome of your solution. This is the "vision of success" that encourages your customer to think about how his or her organization will function after the solutions you recommend are put in place. You can develop many elements of this picture from the concerns the customer has shared throughout your questioning process. Point out how the issues that concern the customer will change after your solution is implemented. If you've asked the right questions and listened carefully up to this point, the vision of success you fashion will closely match the hopes and expectations that motivated your customer to contact you in the first place.

Establishing Value by Defining Your Unique Competitive Advantage

You can't be everything to everyone, no matter how hard you try. It's therefore in your best interest to figure out what you do better than your competitors, and focus your energies there. When you do this sort of self-assessment, you will define an important asset in your sales strategy…your Unique Competitive Advantage. This is a strength you provide, a value you offer, that lets you set yourself apart from others in your market. This strength will be the foundation of your plan for targeting the best market opportunities for your organization. Once you know what you do best, you'll have the information you need to establish and reinforce value for your prospective customers.

If you're not quite sure what makes you unique or sets you apart, try using this simple four-step exercise to help you. You may want to do this exercise at least four times a year (once each quarter) to refresh your thinking about your Unique Competitive Advantage, and how you can use it to help build value with your customers. Ask and answer each of these questions:

1. What makes our center unique?

2. What kinds of programs and promotions are our competitors offering?

3. How can I turn our unique features into benefits for my customers?

4. Which instructors can I use as Subject Matter Experts to describe or demonstrate how our instructional programs apply to the real-world challenges faced by our customers?

Beanisms

Establishing Value – What's the Cost of the Problem?

Sell to your value strengths, not to price

IT training customers would rather buy from higher priced consultative experts than from less skilled salespeople who offer their services at a lower price. For these customers, expertise and proven results are ultimately worth more than the "value" of a lower price. You need to give your customers a lot more than a lower price to differentiate yourself from the competition.

Why? It's simple, really. Most decision-makers in this industry see themselves as exposed and highly vulnerable. They will pay more to reduce or eliminate their risk of failure. If you demonstrate competence and build trust with these customers, you can significantly minimize cost as a barrier to closing the sale.

Know your Unique Competitive Advantage

Build a unique "value added" proposition into your sales strategy that sets you apart from your competitors. Give your customers a clear reason to select you over all the other options available to them. Express this advantage in terms of benefits that are clear and meaningful to your customers.

Establishing value is more than reassurance — it's a matter of proof

You are always wary at first about entering into any commitments with people you don't know well. You have no idea what they can or cannot do. You have no real reason to trust them. As a salesperson dealing with a new customer, either individual or corporate, you should respect this wariness and try to offset it by offering some form of confirmation that your claims about the services you provide are valid.

Win and hold customer mindshare by constantly offering value-adds

When your customers think about IT learning, do they also think about you? When they have questions about IT learning issues, do they turn to you for answers? If so, then you have won mindshare with your customers. They respect your knowledge and understanding in this field, and count on you to help them when they need it.

The key to building mindshare is demonstrating competence and expertise. You can then build on your customer's confidence by offering unexpected value-adds. This can include administrative tools, software enhancements, recommendations on new technology, selected articles and Web-based resources, etc.

Personalize solutions for individual customers

Your individual customers will listen to everything you say, and may nod in agreement with your suggestions. In the back of their minds, however, they're asking, "Yeah, but will this work for me?" Your success with individuals will not depend on how much you impress them with what you've done for others, but with what you demonstrate you can **do** for them.

Chapter 5

Offering the Solution: What's the Right Answer?

The work you've done in Stages 1 and 2 has brought you to this critical point — offering a solution to your customer. This is when you shift the focus temporarily away from the customer's concerns and direct it to you and your capabilities. You've diagnosed the problem, quantified it, and created a vision of how things will be after the problem is resolved. Now, you are ready to describe and explain the solution you recommend. You will also explain why your proposed solution is the right one, and you'll manage any concerns or objections your customer raises. It's now time for MoneyMaker Stage 3 — Offering the Solution.

When working with either individual or corporate customers at Stage 3 in the sales process, your basic tasks are to:

- Propose a workable solution to your customers.
- Close the sale: Gain your customers' agreement with the solution you propose.
- Handle any objections that arise.
- Use value-adds to build trust and good will.

Offering a Solution When Selling to Individuals

Individuals want assurance that the training will work, that it's right for them, that it will help them make a profitable career move. Many will express this desire for value as a concern about price. Because these customers are spending their own hard-earned money, they often cloak their fears about investing in an intangible concept — training — as a price objection. As we'll soon see, when you focus on the real concern — the value of your services, the "what's in it for me?" dimension of the customer's concern — you stand a far better chance of meeting this customer's real need and successfully closing the sale.

Offer the Solution — Closing the Sale

If you've done your job well, you've already invested a lot of time and effort getting to this point. You've asked thoughtful, probing questions. You've analyzed your customer's answers, and processed them against the various options you can provide. The solution you now recommend should be a customized "fit" designed specifically for this customer. It will meet his or her needs not only in terms of content, but also in terms of modality, learning style, scheduling, and degree of difficulty. It will also meet his or her budget of both time and money. The solution will be one that you and your customer hammered out together. It will be a thoughtful plan that matches the best of your capabilities with his or her real needs. Closing this sale is the logical next step.

Your request for the order — the close — should never come as a surprise to your customer. Ideally, your description of your proposal will feel more like a review of information you've already discussed than an introduction of new information. If you've asked appropriate questions throughout the sale and tested your customer's agreement with trial closings, the request for commitment will arrive, without fanfare or anxiety, as the natural and logical last step of your selling process.

While your specific closing question can take many forms, it is almost always framed as a closed question prompting a "yes" answer. For example:

- Is this what you were looking for?
- Have I described a solution that meets your needs and goals?
- Do you think you're ready to move ahead with this program?
- So, what do you think? Are you ready to get started on your new career?
- We have the first course starting next week. Shall I have you enrolled?

Handling Objections: Individuals

In theory, objections to a carefully crafted proposal should be rare. But as every professional salesperson in every field will tell you, they happen. Objections are a natural part of the sales landscape, and your success will often depend on how skillfully you manage these concerns as they arise.

When offering solutions to individual customers, the objections IT training salespeople hear most often revolve around two basic themes:

- Money (or, the lack of it) and
- Time (or, the shortage of it).

In fact, price-related objections are so common that some IT sales professionals will raise the issue even before their customer does. I'm constantly amazed at how many salespeople lead with price before a potential customer even asks for a discount. They seem to do this as a pre-emptive defense against their assumption that the customer will object to the cost of their training services. Needless to say, this is a counterproductive way to build value. As a sales professional offering high quality services, you should always assume that your customer is looking for the best value for his or her money, not necessarily the lowest price in your market. If you know that the value of your training and certification services outweigh their cost, then your task is to demonstrate and clarify this fact to your customer. Never devalue your services and risk diminishing your profit margin by assuming that your customer will object to your prices before he or she raises the issue!

Price-Related Objections

But what happens when the individual training customer does raise a price concern?

Your first response to any price objection should be to change the conversation. This simply means re-focusing your attention onto the practical value that your services provide and the benefits they will offer. When you do this, you're putting the emphasis where your customer really wants it to be, despite any concerns he or she may voice about cost. The most successful salespeople in our business have learned over and over again that individual customers are ultimately much more concerned about figuring out how to build their careers and improve their lives than they are about spending their money. When you place your emphasis on solving that problem, then price is simply what's left over at the end of the day. At that point, price isn't a problem at all. It is simply a part of the solution.

Let's examine the real reasons why our customers raise price objections. There are really only two:

- Either you haven't done enough to build the customers' perception of the value you offer, or

- You haven't helped the customers work out the logistics for financing their investment.

For customer-focused salespeople, these are both manageable challenges.

First, the value objection: You've done your best to build the perception of value, but your customer still tells you your price is too high. What then? First of all, don't panic. Remember that your learning organization has set its prices for good and sound reasons. Quality isn't free, and every learner who walks into your center knows he or she will be getting what he or she pays for. A customer who raises an objection to your price probably knows this too, but may need to be reminded of it.

Then again, you may be dealing with a customer who views every purchasing decision as a challenge to his or her negotiation skills. Consider, for example, one common technique customers use to play the pricing game. Have you ever heard something like this?

> "You know, I spoke to the people at XYZ Technical Training the other day, and they offer a course just like yours for 20 percent less!"

When customers compare your rates negatively to those of your competition, they're usually trying to intimidate you into a "price-matching" strategy. The technique is common enough: You see it every day in the advertising of appliance dealers and electronics warehouses that tell consumers they'll happily meet or beat any other price their customers find. If you were to adopt this approach and match your competitor's prices, it would save your customers money. However, you would also cut directly into your bottom-line profits. And course, you're not selling washing machines or DVD players. You're selling something far more valuable and important, and you may at times need to gently remind your customers of this fact.

For example, you might respond to this sort of price-matching objection with a comment like, "Well, that tells you what they think of their training. Now, let me tell you about what we do here that makes it worth investing a little more in your career."

87

Your bottom line: As a customer-focused sales professional, you should never have to offer price discounts to encourage customers to buy. You will rarely encounter a direct, apples-to-apples comparison between you and your competition in terms of content, method, or teaching style. Your job is to sell on what makes you uniquely valuable to your customers. When those customers really care about the services you offer, they are not looking for, and certainly don't want, the lower priced and lower quality training of a bargain-basement solution.

Handling Price Resistance with Value-Added Incentives

Sometimes, price-related objections arise simply because customers can't comprehend the value of their investment the way they would with something more tangible such as a car, a watch, or a vacation trip. You can take steps to enhance this perception by offering "value-adds" — incentives that increase your customers' perception of the value you offer.

Value-added services or products you could offer to incentivize your customers may take many forms. Some examples include:

- *Free assessment testing to prospective candidates*

  Explain that a pre-test will determine the candidate's current skill levels. This will help ensure that the learner is assigned to a program that's right for him or her. (You may wish to supplement this offer with a recommendation for post-training assessment to evaluate the effectiveness of your training for the learner.)

- *Take-away tools*

  These can include such items as job aids for specific software programs, CDs containing sample tests, or other utilities and reference materials.

- *Discount vouchers*

  Provide certificates offering "free" services, including special programs, testing, etc. (You may wish to encourage your prospects to share these vouchers with their friends who may also be interested in IT training.)

- *Individualized support*

  Offer the learner supplemental instructor mentoring or lab time, as needed, at no extra cost to overcome anxiety, build value, and motivate the reluctant prospect toward a buying decision.

- *Offer a free "retake"*

  If the customer seems anxious about succeeding in your program, respond with an offer of one free guaranteed retake if the learner fails the first effort. This is best offered on a "space available" basis, and with the stipulation that the returning student brings his or her training materials from the first course.

- *Offer "selected" learners access to your labs*

  Access to your center and its technology can be a real bonus for learners who may not have home PCs or opportunities to practice their skills on their corporate systems. This offer is particularly appealing for busy career changers holding full-time jobs.

- *Career counseling*

  Students who are unaware of options available in your local marketplace or who have not made firm career path decisions will welcome any information or guidance you can provide. Of course, you must handle this service with caution. Since career counseling is not your primary skill, you may wish to provide some of your learners with the names or addresses of professional career counselors who can offer skills testing, personality profile testing, counseling and more. Also, consider offering value-added courses designed to assist students with their job search. These can include interviewing skills, effective communication, resume writing, etc.

- *Serve as an information resource*

  Let your prospects know that even after they finish their programs, you will maintain contact to keep them informed about deadlines for re-certification, software updates relevant for them, new training programs, and other pertinent information. In this fast-changing business, you will help them stay on the cutting edge of the technology relevant to them.

This service can be as simple as regular e-mail updates to your current and former students. It not only provides your customers with a trouble-free source of useful career information, but also helps reinforce your organization's mindshare with your graduates. When they find themselves in need of training in the future, the name of your company will still be fresh in their minds because of your regular updates.

- *Networking opportunities*

  Sponsor events that allow your learners to network with other learners and IT professionals. This can be something as simple as an inviting lounge area where students can gather before or after class sessions. You can also encourage contacts among your students, teachers, and other professionals by sponsoring social gatherings. A presentation about trends in IT or new technology releases offered by IT specialists is a natural and productive way to attract graduates, current students, and new prospects to gather and mingle at your training location.

Handling Price Resistance Based on Financing Concerns

As we've seen, many individuals come to organizations like yours because they are unhappy with their current earning power. These customers walk through your door feeling that they don't have enough disposable income, and hoping you can help them get more. While they see the value you offer, they cannot see a way to pay for it within their current budget.

Customers in this situation are common enough that every learning center should have a financing plan in place to help them fund their training. This is both excellent customer service and a practical marketing technique that helps your prospective customers pay for the services you provide.

Many financing options are available to help your students. Some of these include:

- *Provide direct student loans.*

  Some training firms are able to set up independent financing programs for qualified students. By offering self-financed student loans, these companies are able to offer incentives that encourage learners to complete a certain series of related programs.

- *Develop a loan program with a nearby bank or other financial services institution.*

  You may be able to help students obtain financial assistance while avoiding the administrative burden of handling your own program by working with a nearby lending institution. Consider negotiating a relationship with a bank or other facility that can provide funding for your qualified candidates.

- *Learn about and explain government funding programs to your prospects.*

  Direct participants to government agencies, Web sites, or other sources of information about educational loan or scholarship programs sponsored by the government. Be prepared to describe and answer questions about these government programs by educating yourself and preparing for the questions your candidates will most likely ask. Where appropriate, have brochures and application forms available to give to candidates who show interest in these financing opportunities.

- *Suggest blended learning options as money-saving alternatives.*

  For customers working within limited budgets, a customized blended solution may be an ideal short-term solution. Remember that many prospective students may not be aware that IT learning organizations like yours offer much more than traditional ILT (Instructor Led Training) workshops these days. Describe your alternative learning methods, and point out how they can convey knowledge the learners seek within a budget they can afford.

- *Overcome price resistance based on fear of failure.*

  Some customers, especially those who are new to the IT world, may worry that they'll waste their money taking a program that's beyond their abilities. This concern may be expressed in many ways, but their concern usually boils down to one question: "What if I just don't get it?" How you specifically handle this concern is a policy decision for your center. Options may include a free retake policy, one-on-one coaching, individualized testing, and more.

- *Overcome adult learners' anxiety about going back to the classroom.*

  Most adult learners have been out of school for a while, and feel comfortable in the working world. The idea of stepping back into the classroom environment with strangers may be problematic to them for a variety of reasons.

  When you detect this kind of "classroom anxiety," you can help overcome it by offering tours of your classrooms in action. Introduce them to one or more instructors and let them ask questions about the class, the technology, or any other issues that concern them. This experience often helps prospective students realize that your learning environments are nothing like the ones they remember. You can also invite these prospective customers to career nights that bring together your current students with graduates and the corporate representatives who employ them. Of course, you always have the option of providing self-study or blended learning opportunities that can give reluctant students the prerequisite skills they need to reduce or even eliminate their time in the classroom.

Handling Objections to Blended Learning

It's sometimes easy for those of us in the IT training industry to forget that blended learning is still a foreign concept to many of our customers. If you encounter resistance when you recommend a blended learning option, remember that you're probably dealing with fear of the unknown more than anything else. That fear may be expressed by customers with comments like, "I'm just not ready for that" or "E-learning is too scary for me!" or "I've never done anything like that before." An increasingly common objection we hear to e-learning is, "I tried that a couple of years ago, and it was really boring."

You can effectively handle these and other objections using a two-step process of education and support.

First, take some time to educate the customer by describing what blended learning is, how it works, and the results some of your previous learners have achieved using this approach. Answer your prospect's questions and, if appropriate, demonstrate some of the technology that will be a part of your proposed solution. Offering a demonstration of e-learning is a great way to get prospective students excited about the technology and the potential of this learning method.

Second, offer support and assistance to the learner, particularly during the start-up phase of the training. Reassure the student that he or she will have a mentor standing by to help with the first steps into the unfamiliar territory of e-learning, computer-based training, or even self-instructional programming. As the learner progresses, offer coaching services on an as-needed basis. You may even want to set up a "help line" at your offices that learners can call when they have questions or problems working with online or computer-based programs.

Handling Time Resistance with Individual Customers

Almost as common as "I can't afford it" is the objection, "I don't have the time for this."

Time-based objections take many forms: "I'm not ready," "I can't take that much time away from my job/family," "I've got to stay flexible — I can't stick to a fixed schedule," etc. However they express it, customers' time objections are usually based on uninformed assumptions about your schedules and the time commitments they require.

Some specific alternatives to offer individuals with time objections include:

- Blended training options: Design customized paths to fit the schedules of busy learners. Offer a mix of online or CD-ROM based interactive computer learning, hands-on lab sessions, self-study options, mini-workshops, etc.

- Mixed schedules and alternate class times: Does your learning organization offer courses in the evenings? On weekends? At other times when career-changers who currently hold full-time jobs will be available for training? If not, consider developing these flexible program schedules to serve a growing segment of your learner market.

If you've done an effective job defining your prospective learners' needs and wishes up to this point, the objections you hear should not be "show stoppers." As we've seen, they often arise either out of misunderstandings or out of lingering anxiety about life changes that these steps could represent. Remember to always keep your focus, and your customers' attention, on the value they will realize when they achieve their goals. Whether it's a career change, professional advancement, greater marketability in IT, enhanced prestige, or greater personal satisfaction, it is only their perception of value that can ultimately outweigh whatever issues they see standing in the way of their decision to move ahead.

Offering a Solution When Selling to Corporations

The key to successfully presenting and validating a solution to a corporate customer is preparation. All the work you've done up to this point should have developed the facts, the figures, the ideas, and the opinions of the corporate decision-makers to a shared vision of the company's situation, and how you can address it. For corporate customers, you will almost always present your solution by demonstrating its bottom-line advantages for the company. If you've tied your solution to your customer's business plan or to a clearly defined business need, then you will propose a solution that:

94

- Solves business problems that impact the company's bottom line,

- Minimizes the administrative burden on the company while offering maximum flexibility for implementation, and

- Shows a clear, quantifiable, and readily verifiable ROI (one that can be easily explained and verified for upper management as needed).

When you were establishing and reinforcing value in Stage 2, Establishing the Value, you were also clarifying the specifics of the customers' situation. You verified the customers' understanding of their situation using the "trial close" technique. You verified your ability to solve their problems, and obtained their agreement with your early assessments and suggestions. All of this helped you slowly sharpen your focus, leading you toward your recommended solution.

Closing the Sale with Corporate Customers

When presenting your solution to a corporate decision-maker, be sure you do it in a way that makes it easy for that person to say "yes." Your goal, of course, is to facilitate the close by nudging the customer toward a decision he or she should already be prepared to make.

Of course, the simplest way to close is that time-tested rule taught to all salespeople: Ask for the sale. With your pre-work completed, this can be a simple process of asking commitment questions such as:

- Are you ready to move ahead with scheduling the sessions now?

- When do you want to start this training?

- Has this solution I've recommended addressed your problem? Or: Is what I'm proposing in line with what you were looking for?

Another proven technique is the Assumptive Close. This is a statement you make that closes out the customer's "no" option. You assume that the customer has already decided to accept your proposal, and offer him or her two choices for starting the implementation phase.

- Would you prefer to schedule the first group on Monday the 17th, or the following week, on the 24th?

Using Value-Adds to Boost the Corporate Customers' Perception of Value

As we've seen, one of your greatest challenges in today's marketplace is to define and clarify what sets you apart from other training suppliers who are trying to win your customers. What makes you unique? Why would a corporate client decide to do business with you, and not that other training firm down the street? These are some of the critical value-adds that can play an important role at this point in the sales process.

By now, you have already thought about the special features or resources your organization offers to give you a specialized advantage in your market. But is there more you can do to set yourself apart? Of course! Creating value is not just about providing services your customer wants, but about creating the perception of innovative, unique worth in your customer's mind. This is the essence of building value, and this is the essence of winning customer mindshare.

As always, start by putting yourself in your customer's shoes. Ask yourself what you would care about if you were looking for value from an IT training provider. Most corporations today have similar hopes and expectations, so what can you do to address those issues, and how can you do it in a way that sets you apart from others?

Some specific value-adds that training suppliers can provide their corporate customers include:

- *Offer efficiency and flexibility in learning methods.*

  Many corporate customers want a targeted approach to learning that eliminates "frills" and is focused on exactly what their employees need to learn. They also look for flexible schedules that allow their employees to learn whenever they wish. Finally, they want a tailored solution that will provide the training they need within a budget they can afford.

Often, the answer to all these hopes and expectations can be found in a blended learning solution that mixes modalities, scheduling options, and budgetary requirements. We'll be exploring this dynamic learning approach and the advantages it can offer more fully in Chapter 7.

- *Offer to decrease the corporation's administrative role associated with training.*

If it's a given that every corporation wishes to reduce costs, then it is also a given that companies would like to reduce the administrative burden associated with training employees. Scheduling, registration, learner notification, billing, and more are all necessary tasks, but they require an investment of time, money, and resources that chips away at a corporation's profit margin. Can you help your customers by offering to handle some of these tasks as part of the solution package you offer? Consider making some of these core administrative responsibilities a part of your proposal, and be sure to calculate their impact on the customer's potential ROI.

- *Provide outstanding customer service.*

Excellent, personalized customer service is perhaps the easiest value-add you can offer your customers, and yet it is the most often overlooked. Excellent customer service means maintaining and nurturing a caring relationship with the customer. For your corporate clients, this means keeping your customer's long-range plans in mind while always addressing short-term problems and needs as they arise.

On a regular, day-to-day basis, outstanding customer service means treating your customer with respect. Simple courtesies, such as returning phone calls or responding to e-mails promptly, will contribute to the good will your customer feels for you and your organization.

Over the longer term, higher-level customer service may take the form of unsolicited recommendations you make for training options in anticipation of new software releases, certifications, or industry trends. Whatever form it may take, excellent customer service comes down to an attentive mindfulness to your customers, their needs, and the role you can play in helping them achieve their goals.

Handling Common Objections from Corporate Customers

Corporate objections take many forms but, as with individual customers, they typically revolve around issues of time and money. When a corporate customer expresses an objection to any part of your proposed solution, don't try to avoid it or talk your way around it. Meet that objection head on. Start by acknowledging what you've heard. If you have a countering response for the customer's concern, offer it. If you don't, let the customer know that you'll look into the concern, and get back to the customer as soon as possible.

Never leave any objection unanswered! Failing to respond to an objection gives your customer an excuse to reject your offer by assuming that you can't, or won't, answer a particular concern.

Price Objections

A price objection is the corporate customer's way of telling you that you haven't yet developed a clear perception of the cost of the problem, or the value of the solution you're proposing. Some practical options for handling a price objection to a training solution include:

- *Refocus the customer's attention on the quantifiable magnitude of the problem.*

  Has the customer clearly understood the relationship of costs and benefits that you clarified when you calculated the ROI for your solution? Is the problem you propose really solving the issue of greatest concern to the customer? Does the customer understand your proposed solution, and the long-term financial advantages you've proposed? Sometimes, especially during long-term negotiations, you need to remind the customers of the size and cost of their problems to help them remember their value concerns and overcome any anxieties they express about price.

98

- *Suggest creative financing alternatives.*

  Pricing objections sometimes arise with customers who have a pre-determined idea about how they would pay for your IT training services. For example, a manager may visit you with a fixed training budget figure in his or her head, and assume that this number represents a solid barrier that cannot be exceeded.

  Creative financing options you might suggest include tuition reimbursement funds, government programs to help corporations provide training, and tax credits for training. These can all be unexpected sources for corporate funding. Also, has the customer considered looking for alternate funding sources within a project or department budget? If a customer's IT training budget is thin, ask if there are pockets of funding available in other line items of the budget that could be tapped to help fund an IT training and certification initiative.

- *Re-examine your solution — can a lower cost solution solve the problem?*

  You've analyzed the customer's problems and proposed what you know is the right solution — fine. But your customer still tells you there's no way he or she can afford what you've proposed. Do you just give up and walk away from the deal? Of course not. My objective as a salesperson has been and will always be to win every dollar the customer has to spend on training for my company. My customers should never have a reason to spend some of their budget elsewhere, or use available training money for other purposes.

  If the first option you suggest is truly beyond the reach of your corporate customer, consider an alternative, less costly solution that could also solve the training problem. This is a situation where blended learning may provide an effective solution at a lower cost than more expensive traditional learning options.

  Working out these alternatives will take time and effort, but remember: A quick sale may win you short-term gain, but it won't necessarily lead to a long-term business relationship. Keep in mind what we said earlier about excellent customer service and providing that "personal touch" with corporate customers. When you demonstrate your willingness to help your customers find a solution compatible with their budgets, you go a long way toward building trust and confidence in your dedication to solving their problems, not just to making a profit. Corporate customers always recognize this, and always appreciate it. The good will you create with these customers will be an important investment that can pay off for you — big time — down the road.

Time Objections

Corporate objections based on time are often tied to management's concerns about taking employees away from their jobs for training. Managers pressured to meet productivity quotas often resist anything that might stand in the way of their goals. Some practical techniques for handling these concerns include:

- *Provide perspective: Compare the cost of the lack of training and lost productivity due to training downtime.*

  How will your solution help the customer's employees work smarter than they did before? How much more will the employees be able to accomplish in the time available than they could before they were trained? What will that be worth to the customer? How does that number compare to the cost of downtime required for the training solution you propose?

  When you answer these and other questions, you'll help your customers think through a basic cost-benefit analysis for your proposal. This can help the corporate decision-makers see beyond training's short-term impact on productivity to the larger profitability issues that initiated your proposal in the first place.

- *Re-examine your solution: Consider alternatives for time efficiency.*

  If your corporate customer has a problem taking employees off the job for training, have you proposed options to address this issue?

100

Online learning, evening or weekend courses, or take-home self-paced training tools are just some ways you can offer alternatives to the workshop schedules that might eat into corporate productivity. Here again, the options provided by blended learning could open many opportunities for you and your corporate customers that can make their time objections disappear.

LMS (Learning Management System) Objections

Corporate customers who have made a significant investment in a computerized Learning Management System will typically evaluate all new training options through the lens of compatibility. The underlying question these corporate customers ask is, "Will this program work with our system?" or, "Will we need to spend extra money just to make this program compatible with our LMS?"

If you've done effective research along the way, you became aware of the LMS and its issues early in the selling process. Ideally, you were able to integrate information about the LMS into your analysis and proposal from the start. If, however, your customer expresses concerns about how your solution will work with his or her LMS only after you present your recommendation, your challenge becomes a bit different. Steps you can take with this objection include:

- Describe applications with similar systems that you've seen work successfully in other companies. One powerful way to overcome LMS objections is to mention accounts where you have worked successfully with LMS challenges in the past. Describe your experiences, offer written testimonials, or suggest that your prospect contact your satisfied customers directly to learn more about how you handled their LMS issues.

- Offer to help populate the customer's database by interviewing the staff, gathering key data sets, and arranging to have that data entered into the system.

Of course, a response to any LMS objection can only be effective if you, the IT sales professional, are knowledgeable about the features and capabilities of Learning Management Systems. Don't worry…you don't need to study each and every LMS on the market to field your customer's questions. If you familiarize yourself with the top three or four systems now in the market, you should be well prepared to handle most of the questions and issues you'll encounter with your corporate clients.

If you are already familiar with Learning Management Systems and their operation as training support tools, then you are aware of an important caveat for IT training sales consultants: Don't make promises you're not certain you can keep! You may one day be tempted, in your eagerness to close a corporate sale, to tell a corporate customer that you can easily work with his or her existing LMS without clear knowledge that you can. Do not succumb to this temptation! If you do, you may soon find yourself entangled in a serious and expensive problem that could lead to disappointment for your customer, for you, and for your organization.

Your approach to LMS issues or objections should be simple: Don't offer or promise more than you understand, or are certain you can handle. If you need to learn more than you know, tell your customer that you'll be back with a better solution after you do more research and analysis. While this will slow the sales process, your honesty and extra effort will ultimately pay off for both of you in the end.

Corporate Objections Based on Fear

We've described corporate customers as more rational, more fact-driven, and more objective than the individuals who come to you seeking IT training — and they are. But let's not forget that once we get past the corporate veneer, we're dealing with human beings. Like their individual counterparts, corporate customers have their own personal agendas, concerns, and anxieties that inevitably color the decisions or the recommendations they make.

For you, the consultative IT training salesperson, it can be difficult dealing with these corporate anxieties. Unlike your individual prospects, corporate customers rarely talk about their fears or concerns, afraid they might reveal too much about themselves or their anxieties about their role within their organization. If you remain sensitive to some of the more typical fears of corporate training buyers, you can build a solution that addresses those concerns, and nudge your customers toward a positive close.

Some of the more common unspoken concerns that lie behind this kind of reticence include:

- *I'm afraid the training won't go well, and your failure will reflect poorly on me and my decision-making skills.*

    Corporate training projects typically involve many employees. They may require a significant investment of time and money. These and other factors make training a high-visibility undertaking that puts a lot on the line for the person or persons who make the "go" decision. If the project fails or doesn't deliver on its promises, everyone knows it. And, of course, everyone knows where to place the blame.

    When you sense this political anxiety in your corporate representative, start by expressing empathy for his or her concern. Explain that it's natural to be worried about the success of an IT training program, and in fact, you expect wise corporate buyers to expect reassurance that you can deliver what you say you can deliver.

    Then, work on building trust by enhancing and reinforcing the commitments you've made in your solution presentation. Review past successes you've had with companies similar to the customer's company. Provide testimonials or letters of recommendation you've received from other corporate customers. Offer phone numbers of past or current customers who are willing to speak on your behalf. Let your record of success speak for you.

- *Our employees will expect a pay increase or they'll leave for new jobs after we've spent money to train and certify them.*

    This concern is as common among corporate managers as it is undeniable. Yes, sometimes an employee who is trained in one job will decide to leverage those new-found skills into another job that offers higher pay or more prestige. This happens all the time in companies, regardless of whether training is the principal factor motivating the move. A variation on this concern comes up with corporate customers who have purchased expensive e-learning programs in the past only to discover in time that this training was rarely used and failed spectacularly to live up to management's expectations.

When confronting these fears and concerns, your task is to focus the customers' attention on the opportunity that training represents for the corporation, and how that opportunity outweighs the risk it brings in terms of individual employee choice.

Guide your conversation to explore what might happen to the company if its workers are not trained to meet the demands of an increasingly competitive technological marketplace. Explore how an untrained or under-trained workforce can affect the corporation's competitive edge. Then, remind your customer that it will not be just the individual worker who will benefit from this investment — it will also pay off for the corporation in the long run. Then, be prepared to back up these statements with facts and figures from your ROI calculations.

Should a customer remain anxious about this risk of training, consider offering an "insurance policy" that allows the company to recoup its investment loss within a fixed time period.

For example, if a trained and certified employee leaves within six months, you may offer to train and certify another employee free of charge, with the stipulation that the company purchase an upgrade bundle later on. Your offer can include student materials, certification exam vouchers — even the cost of meals! Such gestures of good will demonstrate your understanding of the customer's concern, and your willingness to help him or her deal with it practically and efficiently. Of course, be careful to calculate the potential cost of any such guarantees to your organization before you offer them to customers. Building good will with your corporate customers should never put your bottom line at risk!

Preparing Dynamic Proposals for Corporate Customers

Corporate customers often expect you to describe your solution in a written proposal — a document that describes your recommendations and your costs in detail. A well-prepared proposal obviously takes a lot of thought and careful consideration. However, if you plan ahead, it needn't take too much of your time.

Efficient IT salespeople know that many elements of their proposals are similar from one customer to the next. They take advantage of this consistency by preparing one or more proposal templates that form the foundation for documents that propose specific solutions for individual customers. This is an example of what is called "mass customization" — a process that allows you to create a unique tailored solution for each customer while simultaneously taking advantage of the efficiency we now associate with other automated aspects of business administration.

Traditional written proposals are static documents that seem complete and final. All too often, they attempt to provide a comprehensive solution to every customer problem the salesperson identifies. Zealous salespeople often work hard to dot every "I" and cross every "T," hoping their customers will be impressed by their thoroughness. Often, they're wrong. These comprehensive documents often come across as final and unchangeable recommendations that encourage the customer to reduce everything to a binary Yes/No decision. Wiser salespeople understand two basic realities about preparing corporate proposals:

- First, the chances that the salesperson has gathered every relevant fact and accurately understood every detail of the customer's problem are slim. If you build a final proposal based on what you think you know and understand, you'll probably recommend something inappropriate or flat-out wrong.

- Second, a comprehensive proposal takes a lot more time and effort than a draft or a "work in progress." Why not save yourself the work of dreaming up a comprehensive but imperfect solution when you can save time and increase your chances of success by submitting a first draft instead?

Set the stage before presenting your proposal by telling the corporate decision-maker that your document will be a draft submitted for review and mark-up. It is not a final recommendation for approval. To underscore this point, consider adding the words FIRST DRAFT to the document footer, or as a watermark behind the text. Position your draft proposal as only a preliminary collection of thoughts and ideas. Ask your customer to review this document with a critical eye, editing it to correct your mistakes, provide insight, and offer an informed perspective on your ideas. Encourage the customer to actively participate in the development process by saying something like, "I'll e-mail you my draft so you can look it over. I'll give you a call to ask what you liked and where you think I'm off base."

From your corporate customers' point of view, this approach gives them the opportunity to make your proposal more relevant, more practical, and more productive. From your point of view, you are helping your customers to sell themselves by making them partners and co-creators of your proposal.

A draft proposal also allows you to present a series of trial closings that can test your client's responsiveness to your ideas, or uncover needs and preferences you might have missed. After you receive feedback from your prospect, you should have little trouble preparing a revised version of your document that incorporates new ideas and recommendations based on the changes your client suggests.

By the time you send your customer or prospect the final draft of your proposal, your customer should already be sold, and ready to close. After all, he or she helped create the solution you are recommending. Try it! You'll be surprised how often your customers will complement you on your insight and excellent service without ever realizing how much of the work is actually their own.

One final word about formal proposals prepared for corporate clients: If you're like most of us, sooner or later you will be asked to write a proposal for a prospect who has no intention of buying your IT training services. The only purpose in asking you for a bid is to leverage a lower price from another company he or she has already decided to hire. This, of course, is a terrible waste of your time and an abuse of your professionalism. But it does happen.

Another frustrating situation we IT training salespeople encounter is the prospect who unintentionally misleads us by requesting a proposal when all he or she really wants is a simple price quote. These customers have no devious or manipulative intent. They are simply poor communicators who are unclear about what they want. Such a miscommunication, however, can still waste a lot of your valuable time and effort.

How can you protect yourself from these situations? How do you avoid wasting your time on proposals that are guaranteed to go nowhere? First, of course, is to be aware that these circumstances exist, and be on the lookout for them. If you suspect that your client may be positioning you for a leveraging proposal or is only looking for a price quote, ask some questions that may help surface, or at least hint at, the client's real intentions.

Examples of such questions include:

- What is your timeframe for making this decision?
- Has the budget been identified for this project?
- What are the criteria you'll be using to make your decision on this proposal?
- Which is more important to you, lowest price or overall value?
- Are we a serious contender for this business?

A Note About Failure: Dealing with the Lost Sale

Common sense tells you that there will be times when you work hard to win a corporate account, but come up empty. No salesperson on earth successfully closes every sale, and you too will have the experience of losing out now and then. Since this is an inevitable part of the sales landscape, ask yourself, "What can I learn from these experiences that will help me do a better job in the future?" Every sale you attempt to make, especially the losses, can be a valuable learning experience if you don't just shrug them off as a wasted effort. Some ideas for ways to turn these lemons into potentially valuable lemonade include:

- *Complete a lost sale analysis.*

  Have you ever taken the time to ask a corporate prospect why you lost a sale? A quick phone call to the prospect after you receive word that the account you wanted went to a competitor can teach you a lot about your customer's expectations, your competitor's marketing strategy, and the weaknesses perceived in your proposal.

  Remember that the customers probably made their decision on objective criteria, not emotional fondness for one training supplier over another. They will usually be very open and honest with you, and will probably respect you more for caring about how they made their decision. You may learn that you didn't ask enough questions, or ask the right questions. Perhaps you impressed everyone you met, but you never really got to speak with the final decision-maker. Whatever the cause, these short "post-mortem" interviews can help you modify and fine-tune your presentations to avoid repeating the mistakes that cost you the business you worked so hard to win.

- *Maintain a relationship with the prospect.*

  All right, your competitor came out on top in your head-to-head competition for a corporate training account. But will he or she be able to hold onto it? Winning an account is one thing, maintaining it is something else. If your competitor isn't able to live up to the promises he or she made during the sales phase, the client may anxiously look about for an alternate solution to the problem. Who better than someone who's already demonstrated the ability and willingness to handle the job — you? When you first learn that you lost a sale, offer to serve as a back-up resource for the customer should the need arise.

Contact the client with a short note or e-mail at regular intervals to remind him or her of your continuing interest in serving his or her training needs. Be sure to mention any new programs or services your organization offers in these messages. When you make it your business to stand in the wings with your prospective customers, you position your organization not only to win an account but also to win long-lasting good will when you step in to save the day for a customer who's been let down by another supplier of IT training.

- *Clarify your customer's perception of your service gaps.*

  Once you learn the reason why you lost a sale, you've uncovered the basic gap between what your customer wanted and what you proposed. Ask the customer to clarify how your competitors were able to fill that gap. Your goal here is to find out what contract-winning services or value-adds your competitors are providing that you are not. Once you find out, take the steps you need to fill that gap in your offerings so it never costs you another corporate sale.

- *Shop your competition.*

  The Internet has made it easy and convenient to research your competitors' offerings and pricing structure. Remain aware of what your competitors are doing and what special offers they're making. If you want a more thorough assessment of your competitors and their capabilities, consider assigning members of your sales team to visit their centers, speak with their sales reps, and even sign up for classes. This sort of in-depth evaluation can give you a clear picture of what you're up against, and help you develop an effective strategy for positioning yourself against both the strengths and the weaknesses of their operation.

Beanisms

Offering the Solution – What's the Right Answer?

Closing the sale should be a natural extension of the selling process

Your request for the order should never come as a surprise to your customer. If you've asked appropriate questions throughout the sale and tested the customer's preliminary agreement with trial closings, the request for commitment will arrive, without fanfare or anxiety, as the natural and logical last step of your selling process.

When you're hit with an objection, try to change the conversation

If your customer tries to focus your discussions on how expensive your services are or why your proposal just won't work, change that focus to value. Demonstrate what you will do to support their business through value-added service, products, sales training, seminars, assessment products, etc. Change the center of gravity from, "Here's how you can buy from us" to "Here's how we can help you grow your business or solve your problem."

The two most common objections to IT training are money and time

Customers will tell you that they don't have the money to pay for your services or they'll complain that they don't have the time to complete the training you've planned. Don't try to argue these points. Instead, change the focus to emphasize the value benefits of your solution. Then, as needed, offer your customers alternate resources for funding or flexible scheduling options that can overcome the logistical problems they may face.

Be prepared to help individual customers explore financing options

If money problems are a common issue for your customers, it only makes sense to be ready for their objections with proposals and options to help resolve these problems. Whether you offer an independent loan program, a relationship with a private lending institution, information about government loan programs, or some other resource, the most important point here is to have practical options available that the customers can explore to help get them moving forward with the programs you recommend.

Turn every lost sale into a learning opportunity

Losing a sale is part of the game for every salesperson. These losses don't have to be entirely negative experiences. You can salvage tangible benefits from lost sales by learning lessons from the experience, and then keeping your options open for future sales opportunities with the prospect.

Begin by simply calling the customer and asking why you lost the sale. More often than not, he or she will tell you. Listen to why he or she didn't buy from you. Don't be angry or defensive. Learn from it, and correct your sales strategy or service offering. At the end of the day, that is what being an effective competitor is about.

Maintain your relationship with the prospect no matter how disappointed you are. Keep in mind that the vendor who beat you may disappoint the customer. You should stay ready to pick up the ball if your competitor should drop it.

Make your corporate proposals dynamic, working documents

Before you present a written proposal to corporate decision-makers, advise your customers that your document is a first draft for their review and mark-up — not a final proposal to be accepted or rejected. To underscore this point, you may wish to add the words FIRST DRAFT in the footer or as a watermark. Encourage the customers to take partial ownership of the proposal by asking them to tell you what they like and don't like.

Chapter

Building on
Success:
Upselling

6

"You want fries with that?"

For many of us, the image of a bored teenager saying these words while taking our fast food order captures the essence of upselling — and it's not a pretty picture. We think of upselling as something retailers do to maximize their profits. "This tie would sure look great with that new shirt, sir!" But you didn't really come into the shop looking for a tie, did you? "With that new computer you're buying, we're offering a store service package that will protect you against any problems for three years…for only this much more!" But you thought you already knew how much you'd be spending….

And so it goes. Just when you're feeling good about making one purchase, you're pressured to make another one. You feel manipulated, not served. You wonder if the salesperson might be playing some sort of perverse game whose object is to get the highest score by extracting as much money out of you as possible.

Experiences like these can leave us uncomfortable and feeling vaguely used. After all, we've already agreed to do business with someone. What should we think when the very next thing they do is try to build their profit by selling us something else? This seems to fly in the face of customer-focused, needs-based selling. It's not really surprising, then, that some sales professionals are uneasy about upselling, and the connotations it seems to carry.

Upselling as Education

This wariness might be justified were it not for one fundamental fact about our industry: As you know, the IT marketplace is an ever-changing work in progress. No one — especially your customers — can ever keep up, and know everything there is to know. As an IT education professional, you are the expert, the analyst, the authority whom your customers depend on for updated information and the right educational recommendations. Your customers expect you to assess their needs and match those needs to the newest capabilities of the IT marketplace and the latest innovations in training methods.

When you recommend new learning opportunities to your customers, you do it because you understand, and can carefully explain, the advantages that a specific training or certification option can provide. For example, a learner who has learned the fundamentals of microhardware and desktop operating systems in an A+ certification program is a logical upsell candidate for a Network+™ certification that takes him or her into the fundamentals of networking. You know IT.

You know trends in business and industry. You know training. And you know the latest educational modalities for teaching IT skills. Who is better qualified than you, the IT training professional, to recommend the best program suggestions for your learners?

As you work through this process, you'll often find yourself making recommendations your customers didn't expect. On the surface, this might seem like the kind of upselling we described earlier. In fact, it is fundamentally different.

The informed recommendations you make are a form of education, not manipulation. You are suggesting an opportunity your customer would never have considered without your informed guidance. You are most assuredly not flogging unnecessary add-ons to build your profit margin. In fact, if you do your job well, this educational process will be an integral part of all your customer contacts, and will become a basic element in your customer-focused selling approach. It is this process of informed consultation and personalized guidance that we're referring to when we speak of "upselling," the fourth stage of our selling process.

From your point of view, the advantages of upselling should be obvious: An upsale to an existing customer is much easier than a first-time sale. Why? Because you already know your existing customers, and they know you. The hard spadework is already done. You've gathered basic data about the customers and their needs. These customers already have experience with your services and methods, so they've overcome any anxieties they may have had about you. If you've done a good job for them, making additional sales to these customers should be an easy and natural part of your sales cycle.

And yet we know that so many of us fail to take advantage of these opportunities! Researchers in this field tell us that between 80 and 90 percent of all technical training firms have no established plans for developing new business from current or former customers. We seem to prefer spending our time and energy seeking out new business while overlooking opportunities to sell to the customers we already have.

If we think about this, we realize that this odd tendency among us sales types is neither logical nor efficient. Consider: If you've already qualified your customer and proven your value as a training supplier, doesn't it make sense to build on that success by selling this same customer something new? These customers are the "low-hanging fruit" of the training business. We do our company and ourselves a favor when we develop these customers into ongoing, long-term business partners.

For IT trainers, the essence of upselling is tilling the soil you've already cultivated in a new way that benefits everyone. When working at Stage 4, Upselling, your basic tasks are to:

- Identify add-on opportunities that are appropriate to the learner's needs.

- Lay the groundwork for future sales.

- Ask for referrals and leads, either internal or external.

Working with Readymades: Why Upselling Makes Sense for Profit-Minded Salespeople

Upselling sets the stage for a partnership with customers by building a bridge between the end of one sales cycle and the beginning of another. Upselling, as we've seen, is often much easier and more time-efficient than cold-call selling. The existing customers we approach for upsells are no longer prospects, but "readymades" — that is, they've been qualified, their needs have been identified, and they're satisfied with your track record of success. These readymades are golden opportunities for you and your organization — so long as you make the effort to reach out for them.

Pursuing readymade upselling opportunities begins when you ask yourself:

- Do we offer other classes or certifications that would benefit this customer?

- Are there add-ons we can offer that would enhance this customer's current training package?

- Are there any new technologies to be implemented?
- Is the customer planning any system upgrades for the near future?
- Are there any new IT projects or planned upgrades the customer may be thinking about for the future?
- Do I know of any new training or certification opportunities being introduced that would be right for this customer?

Laying the Groundwork for Future Sales

As with so many aspects of this consultative selling process, the best way to upsell is through preparation. Be organized about pursuing readymade opportunities by establishing an "action plan" that includes checking on the future training needs of your customers.

Know when your students will complete their current training, and think through what they've told you about their career paths and what they hope to do with their new skills and enhanced earning potential. Then, talk to these students about their next logical steps toward their goals.

For some, this will be something as obvious as moving from a basic skill development session to an intermediate level program. For others, it may mean broadening their skills base into a related subject area to build competency or earn a certification. Make sure to clearly describe any class you recommend, and when the next session will begin. Then, be sure to ask the student if you can reserve a place in that session for him or her.

Reaching Out to Your Alumni

If you're like me, you probably receive regular correspondence from the college or university you attended, no matter how many years ago that may have been. Why are they doing this? Are they sentimentalists, wistfully remembering the days when you bounded across the campus with your jaunty step? Of course not! They're hoping you will be sentimental enough about your college days that you'll write them a check.

119

These academic institutions know well the value of their alumni lists — and so should you. Make sure your educational organization has a system for keeping in touch with the students you train after they graduate from your programs. Keep these graduates informed about new technology as it is released, and encourage them to pursue a path of life-long learning and renewal. Invite your graduates back to your offices so they can see and expose themselves to new products as they become available. Let them know that you feel obligated to keep them up-to-date and on the cutting edge of the newest technological developments and trends.

When a new certification or a recertification is released, tell your former students about it. Keep them abreast of these developments. You may wish to offer a small reduction in price as an incentive for recertification to students who earned their initial certifications with your firm.

Do you now offer accelerated classes or blended learning options to attract former students who learned the basics in your workshops? These experienced students, like some of your newer prospects, will benefit from a tailored solution customized to fit their needs. This kind of personalized service will go a long way toward building alumni mindshare as you provide excellent ongoing service and follow-up — the kind of service that's rare enough these days to be surprising and delightful when it occurs!

Strategies for Upselling Individuals

Don't let a workshop, certification seminar, or e-learning program end without meeting with the students to discuss their appropriate next steps. Are you prepared for these meetings? Do you have brochures or leaflets prepared that outline the curriculum offerings you'll recommend? As we've seen so often before, a little pre-planning can go a long way toward making the next sale easier and much more effective.

But the completion of a course or program is certainly not the only option available to you for upselling your individual learners. As we've seen, a contact list of your former students can be a rich resource for prospective repeat business if you till that soil carefully.

Your client contact database should include all the basic information about your current and past clients. At a minimum, that means:

- The learner's name
- The learner's business contact information, including e-mail address
- The learner's training goals/objectives
- A list of all courses completed and now under way
- A list of certifications passed

Of course, you can supplement this basic information with other useful data as you see fit. For example, you may want to record answers to questions like:

- Where were they hired, when, and into what position?
- Have they received any specialized training from their employer?
- What are their funding sources?
- How are they doing? (Are they happy in their job? Expecting a promotion? Searching for something new?)
- Have they earned any new certifications?

The specific data categories you maintain are up to you, but no matter what you decide to track, be sure to keep your records current. The only truly valuable database is an accurate and timely compilation of your learner records. An out-of-date list can be frustrating and, in some situations, worse than useless.

Use your student database to stay in touch with your graduates. Keep them informed about new training programs you introduce, new certifications made available by vendors or independent organizations, new training modalities, and more. Your student database can also identify those whose learning path or skill set makes them likely candidates for your newest offerings.

Send these prospects targeted mailings (either electronic or standard) to alert them to your new offerings, and consider adding a financial incentive offered only to your "valued alumni." Use these mailings to keep these prospects up-to-date about vendor announcements, system upgrades, and new certification requirements. Is something new being released? Are certification requirements being upgraded or changed? Let everyone in your database know about these developments if they might possibly benefit from this information.

You can also provide a practical value-added service to your former students by serving as an informal job center for selected students. This can be as simple as calling a graduate to let him or her know when you hear about career opportunities that are right for him or her, or sharing information about students when a company calls you looking for qualified candidates to fill IT positions.

Upselling Through Alumni Gatherings

Have you ever invited your former students back for a reunion or special event sponsored just for them? You and your organization can gain a lot by holding these gatherings at your offices, where guests can mingle, network, learn about your newest programs, and even get a little hands-on practice with your latest e-learning tools. These events can also let you promote upcoming classes or special events.

Some IT learning firms have won significant repeat business from individual customers by sponsoring informational events built around demonstrations of newly released technology or talks about industry trends by IT experts. When you promote these special events as free value-added benefits for past and present learners, you create a "win-win" for everyone. Your guests will appreciate being kept up-to-date on the latest developments in IT technology as well as the opportunity to visit with old friends and acquaintances.

Upselling Through Your Instructors

Your ILT students spend most of their time in the classroom or lab facilities where their training takes place. Your instructors have far and away the greatest amount of contact time with your students — certainly more than you or others on your sales staff. This means that your instructors can be one of your most potent resources for upselling. Then why not enlist them in the upselling process?

First, make sure your trainers are aware of the role they can play. Let them know that they really can make a difference in how many students they train by becoming an active part of your marketing strategy. Then, prepare them for their role by making sure they are informed and up-to-date on your latest offerings. Encourage them to inform their students about the breadth and depth of your educational opportunities. You may wish to offer financial incentives to trainers who successfully encourage participants to sign up for additional programs. Of course, your instructors should then refer any students to you or other sales specialists when they show interest or ask for more information about a program.

Some proactive steps you can take to involve your instructors include the following:

- Make sure that brochures, leaflets, or other printed marketing materials are available in classrooms, break areas, and other locations in your learning center. Ask instructors to distribute targeted brochures for logical follow-up classes or special events, and have them occasionally remind students about the other materials that are available. Instructors can also use the available information technology tools themselves to upsell your programs by directing students to Web sites designed to provide tools and program information for students.

- Ask instructors to describe your curriculum to their ILT classes at the beginning and again at the end of a workshop. Have them focus on programs relevant to the learner group. For example, a basic networking session would be a logical place to describe intermediate and advanced sessions on networking.

123

- Invite instructors to join your sales discussions with prospects. Ask these instructors to describe their training methods or philosophies, answer the prospects' IT questions, and generally offer added perspective on the benefits and capacities you offer.

- Educate your instructors about recommended learning paths for students seeking various certifications. Encourage them to counsel and recommend appropriate classes to the students working toward these certifications.

- Ask instructors to contribute features for your newsletters or other updates sent to former and current students. Take advantage of their experience and knowledge to help your student base stay informed about IT trends and training opportunities.

- Recruit your best instructors to deliver special promotional programs such as "lunch-and-learn" mini-sessions on popular technical topics.

Asking for Referrals from Individual Customers

If you're like most of us, your best and most productive sources of prospects for future business are referrals you get from your current customers. Common sense tells us that an individual or a company now doing business with us probably knows about others who would benefit from our services. For individual customers, you can take advantage of this resource by making a point of asking if they know of friends or associates who would benefit from your training services.

When is the best time to prospect for new leads by asking for referrals? More often than you probably imagine! Virtually any contact situation with your current individual students may be right for a referral request. Some of the occasions that can be converted into fruitful referral opportunities include:

- After any successful close when the customer has agreed to purchase training services.

- During an initial meeting with a prospective customer.

- After a first workshop or lab session.

- During the lunch or coffee breaks of training classes.

- While making a presentation or special offer over the telephone.

How you ask for referrals can vary as widely as the circumstances in which you ask. This request should not stand out in any way. Instead, frame it as a simple question that you weave smoothly into the fabric of your conversation. Simple referral requests can take many different forms, including:

- Do you know anyone else at your company who might benefit from this training the way you did?

- Do you have any co-workers at your office who might also benefit from this program?

- You've talked about your friend Susan a lot. Do you think she'd enjoy this program as much as you have?

The payback from referrals such as these can be tremendous. When a learner has a good experience with an IT learning organization, he or she is often eager to pass on information about it, and share that success with others. You're virtually assured that the leads you get will be "hot" prospects. They have, after all, been pre-qualified by someone who already knows you, your organization, and your capabilities. Much of the work that occupied you in Stage 1 of the selling process is done for you!

There's no single "best" time in your relationship to ask for this information, but a good rule of thumb is to ask when you know your customer is happy. When you see and hear expressions of satisfaction and enthusiasm about your programs, ask your satisfied customers if they know anyone else who might want to share their success.

If it seems appropriate, you may consider asking your students to personally contact the persons they're referring to let them know you'll be calling. This lets your students give you an initial "seal of approval" with the prospects. It helps establish your credibility and trustworthiness right from the start. Then, when you first contact the prospective customers, you'll be ideally positioned to identify opportunities, build trust, and demonstrate the value of your services.

Strategies for Upselling Corporations

Ideally, your goal with every corporate customer is to establish an ongoing partnership that will position you as the solution of choice for the company's training needs as they evolve over time. Upselling is a natural element in developing and nurturing such relationships. It allows you to link your corporate training solutions together into a seamless web of learning. Corporate upselling, like upselling for individuals, is about educating the customer about opportunities and options to build the most efficient and cost-effective training solutions possible.

Upselling to corporate customers consists of:

- Seeking and identifying opportunities for appropriate add-on sales.
- Preparing the groundwork for future sales.
- Requesting referrals from both inside and outside the corporation.

After you have proposed a solution and closed a sale with a corporate customer, you may have several opportunities to suggest appropriate add-ons or additional opportunities. These might include:

- Additional classes to complement the primary training. Suggest that those classes could be integrated into the company's current training package.
- Certifications that would be logical outcomes for the training paths purchased by your corporate customer.

  Review the benefits of certification, and explain how many qualifications and requirements the learners will meet when the proposed training is complete. Then suggest adding formal certification as an additional goal of the package. If the customer agrees, modify the basic training package to fully meet the certification requirements.

- Advising customers accustomed to ILT training about e-learning or lab opportunities you offer that would enhance their learning experience.

- Mentioning any specials or discounts currently available from your learning organization that can be worked into your customer's training package.

Customer Service for Corporate Accounts: The Art of Being There

If you offer excellent customer service to your corporate clients, you're already well on your way toward successful upselling. That's because the foundation of great service for corporate customers is simply being available — staying in touch, staying on top of the latest developments, and being responsive to the company's needs as they arise. That's logical enough, isn't it? If you're regularly in contact with your customers, answering their questions and helping them solve their problems, you are ideally positioned to sell additional solutions when new training needs are identified.

Effective follow-up to maintain this contact with corporate customers, like so much else about selling, should be planned. Be sure to build structure into your contact strategy by establishing a schedule for following up with key corporate decision-makers.

For example, some IT trainers plan direct contacts with each of their corporate customers at least once every thirty days. Some larger firms categorize their corporate accounts by account size, calling on "A" list prospects once a week, "B" list accounts once a month, and "C" list clients once every two or three months. Whatever contact strategy you decide is right for you, give it a try and follow through with it. Use your company's database or LMS to sort, organize, and process the essential contact information you collect and make your job a lot easier. If you're like others who've applied this structured approach to their client contacts, you should find that it often leads to very positive results.

Make it a point to establish several personal contacts within your corporate accounts to gain a broader understanding of the issues surrounding technology deployment in the company. Regular face-to-face visits with IT managers, training managers, and Human Resource Development (HRD) executives, as well as upper-level management, will give you a chance to build good will while also gathering background data for your future proposals.

Some IT training consultants find they can learn a lot about their corporate clients by simply sharing a casual lunch with employees in the corporate cafeteria. This short visit with front-line workers, system operators, and others who use the company's IT systems can offer insights into what's working and what isn't, and where IT training might make a difference for the better. By "being there" in this way, these salespeople sometimes gain insights they'd never find in an executive conference room.

While your corporate accounts take time and effort to develop, there are many ways you can make your visits and other contacts as efficient as possible. Consider these ideas to help ensure that your face-to-face contacts with corporate customers yield maximum value for you and your customers:

- *Status checks and needs reviews*

  Schedule a meeting with your customers to survey the effectiveness of the recent IT training you provided for their employees. Use this meeting to probe for any other knowledge gaps in the learner base. Ask questions like:

  - How well do you think this training met the group's needs or expectations?

  - From your point of view, how well do you think we did at meeting your organizational objectives we agreed to before we began this process?

  - Do any training graduates need remediation? Mentoring? Coaching? (If yes, be prepared to recommend a solution.)

  - Have any new needs or problems arisen since the training session that technical training might resolve?

- *Informational meetings for technology and training updates*

  Plan sessions with your corporate contacts billed as value-added IT updates. Share information you gain about new system technologies, training methodologies, assessments, certifications, or other areas relevant to the corporation's interests. During these meetings, be sure to ask questions like:

  - How do you think these new software (or hardware) releases may impact the company's business?

  - Do you have specific plans to introduce new technology in the near future that may create additional training needs?

  - What can we do together that will help your company prepare for the next wave of the IT revolution?

- *Business reviews — quarterly, bi-annual, or annual assessments*

  Formal business reviews can be scheduled with corporate decision-makers to do a comprehensive assessment of your relationship with the customer. These reviews allow you to analyze results, receive feedback, evaluate the effectiveness of your programs, and develop long-range goals. They may include a formal cost/benefit analysis that your contacts can use to validate their investment in training to upper-level management.

  The business review can be a valuable tool for cementing your long-term partnerships with corporate clients. It formalizes a feedback mechanism to ensure that you are meeting your customers' expectations, and will respond quickly if any problems are identified.

  Questions to ask during a business review may include:

  - How have your internal numbers matched up against the ROI projections we made before the training began? (Note: Be sure to do your homework before asking this or similar questions by developing your own answers, from your perspective, beforehand.)

  - Are all your system users effective and up-to-date on relevant applications?

- How well did the training transfer to the workplace and help improve employee performance since the training took place?

- Does current staff performance meet or exceed the ROI specifications you calculated during the "Establishing Value" phase of the selling process?

- Is the company satisfied with its current ROI for information technology systems and personnel?

- *Transparency: Providing corporate customers with e-access to your training results*

  You will build added trust and good will with some corporate clients by implementing an Internet-based system that allows selected corporate decision-makers to review the progress of their trainees, dynamically track their return on investment, and coach any employees who may be struggling with the program. Managers, trainers, and others with a vested interest in your training will be able to check in "real time" on how well individuals or groups perform in your programs. By openly sharing this information, you will assure your corporate customers that you are working in open partnership with them. You'll also provide further evidence that you are a working partner interested in developing effective productivity solutions for your customers.

- *Soliciting feedback: Evaluating your performance*

  As you evaluate your corporate customers' training needs, you can also demonstrate your respect for your customers and their opinions by asking them to evaluate you, your company, and the services you provide. Many successful salespeople consider this an empowering technique to build customers' trust and confidence in their organization.

  Feedback can be gathered in question-and-answer sessions after workshops. You can also provide an evaluation checklist or worksheet that corporate learners and decision-makers can use to tabulate their views. However you gather this information, this review process enhances your relationship by letting your customers know that you value their opinions as well as their business. This gesture says, "We respect and value you enough to ask you for advice on how we can improve the way we provide service to customers like you."

If your customers have been happy with your training, their evaluation also invites them to affirm the difference you've made for their company, and to offer ideas on ways you might help them even further. In other words, it invites the customers to suggest your next upsell opportunity!

Asking your corporate customers to evaluate your IT training can be a no-lose proposition for you and for your organization. Sure, there's always risk you may hear things you don't want to hear. But wouldn't it be better to hear negative feedback on your terms at a time when you might correct the problem rather than later, when the customer decides to solve the problem by finding a new training vendor? Don't let anxiety about possible criticism stand in the way of this excellent opportunity to solve problems, build trust, and forge good will between you and your corporate clients.

- *Remember the basic customer service rule: Under-promise and over-deliver*

  The best way to provide excellent customer service for your corporate clients is to "under-promise and over-deliver." If you stick to this principle, you'll stand out from the majority of salespeople working to win business today, who try to gain competitive advantage by promising as much as possible — if not more — to win the business. Of course, the problem with that approach is that once you've won the business, you're faced with the challenge of delivering on your promises. If you fail to do this, if things do not run smoothly, your chances of winning repeat business with the customer will diminish rapidly. You can control your customer's perceptions by setting expectations early in your relationship that will prevent over-commitment and keep you from making promises you can't keep.

  An effective way to protect yourself from over-committing is to promise less than you know you can handle, and then provide more than you say you will. In training organizations, this may

131

be difficult or impossible to do without the active involvement of others. You may wish to confer closely with those responsible for scheduling workshops and lab time, registration, assigning instructors, and conducting the training to specify what can and cannot be safely promised to a customer. To safeguard your organization against over-commitment, consider setting up a process that allows all critical parties to review and sign off on the corporate training proposals you develop. This care is particularly important when you are delivering unique customized events or delivering a training program on-site for a customer.

The easiest way to disappoint any corporate customer is to fail to deliver on your promises. This means, for example, that you should never cancel a scheduled training session, no matter how difficult it may be to make it happen. Remember that, for your customer, someone may have given up a vacation or rescheduled a project to make the time for your class. Corporate decision-makers may have argued to justify your training event, winning the debate only after putting their necks on the line with higher management. Imagine how they'd feel if they were to show up only to find that you'd cancelled the session at the last minute? What do you think your chances would be of getting more business from this company? NEVER disappoint your customer by failing to deliver on your commitments!

Asking for Referrals from Corporate Customers

When you and your organization have done a good job for a corporate customer, your contacts become a natural and rich resource for new sales leads. When your customer is pleased with you and your training services, take advantage of that enthusiasm by:

- *Asking for a peer referral within the organization*

  Are there other departments, divisions, or project groups within the company that could benefit from your training services? You will facilitate your penetration within a company by first asking for potential leads, and then requesting an introduction by your contact. An introductory "hand-off" from your contact will give you a starting topic of conversation with the prospect as you describe the successes you've already had within the organization. Your initial contact can also provide independent testimonials about the value you offer.

- *Asking for a referral outside the organization*

  Corporate customers don't live in plastic bubbles. The managers and trainees you meet in corporate settings all have friends and associates who work at other companies, and all of them face the same basic challenges as your customers. These people also have friends and colleagues through their memberships in industry associations or other inter-corporate groups. If these people can benefit from your training services, why not ask your satisfied customers to help you contact them?

  Your corporate customers who truly value your training organization will be happy to tip their friends off about such a valuable resource. Be ready to take advantage of your customers' networking potential by pointedly asking for these outside referrals. Don't assume that your customers might be unwilling or fearful about "sharing" a valued resource with another company. Remain positive, and assume that your satisfied corporate customers will gladly pass on to their friends the same good fortune that came their way when they first met you!

- *Asking for referrals during telesales calls*

  With only a little extra effort, you can significantly leverage your telesales calls to prospective customers by asking one extra question — "Do you know anyone else who might be interested in this offer?" This request can help you regardless of how the prospect responds to your initial offer. If he or she is not interested, he or she may find it easier to say "no" to you by offering the name and number of a friend or associate as a "consolation prize." You have nothing to lose and everything to gain by asking the question — so why not just ask?

- *Asking for referrals at the conclusion of training or certification sessions*

  Your students typically feel the most satisfied and positive about their training experience right after they successfully finish a training session or earn a certification. This moment — when your students are feeling great about your programs or when they return to the workplace and you have the opportunity to speak with the decision-maker — is an ideal time to request a referral.

- *Asking decision-makers for referrals when they visit an ILT classroom session*

  Key decision-makers often drop in on program sessions to monitor the class and get a sense of how things are going. If the session meets or exceeds the learners' expectations, take a moment during a break to ask the decision-maker for referrals. If you've heard good comments about the session from some of the students sponsored by this decision-maker, be sure to share those opinions before asking for the referral, to build value for the customer.

- *Asking students for referrals during breaks, over lunch or dinner, etc.*

  A break, whether for a quick cup of coffee or a meal, is a time when instructors and students usually relax and converse more casually than they do on the job or in a formal program setting. This setting provides a great opportunity to ask broad-ranging questions about systems technology, and about the training needs of friends or co-workers for the training services you offer. Pursue referrals by asking for a name and number — and don't forget to ask if you can use the name of the person who made the referral when you make your first contact with the prospect!

The referral requests you make will, of course, be phrased in a way that's comfortable for you, but some examples of effective referral questions that you could re-word to fit your needs include the following:

- Do you know anyone else who you think could use this kind of training?

- This is really a great promotion, and I'm glad you're taking advantage of it. Who else do you know who might want to take advantage of this special offer?

- I'm so glad to hear you say that this course was a good learning experience for you. Do you know anyone else who might enjoy learning about the new features available in this latest release of this program?

- At break today, I heard you mention that one of your co-workers has a big project coming up that'll be using this same software that we're teaching next month. Would it be OK with you if I gave her a call to tell her about these courses we have coming up?

As we've been saying all along, the MoneyMaker sales model is a consultative approach to selling in the IT training business. Consultancy in selling is a more complex, back-and-forth process than simply presenting and closing. You must gather and filter information to service your customers by matching their needs to the solutions you can provide. In this context, asking for referrals becomes one more technique for developing the information you need to serve your customers — all your customers — as effectively as possible.

Using Incentives

A referral given to you by a satisfied corporate customer can be worth a lot to you — but isn't it terrific that referrals themselves are free? You may wish to thank your customers for their referrals by rewarding them in small ways for their help. The incentives you provide should be as innovative and original as you are. Some ideas that IT trainers have used for referrals in the past include:

- Money (the universal incentive!)
- Free access to "Ask the Expert" technical consultants
- Testing vouchers
- T-shirts, coffee mugs, pens, etc.

And don't forget to incentivize your instructors as well. If your trainers successfully encourage students to sign up for other programs, they should also be recognized for their marketing success. This recognition can take many forms: A commission for closed sales, dinner certificates for an elegant restaurant, an "Instructor of the Month" award, or some other recognition will tell trainers that you appreciate their help in building the business. It will also encourage them and their peers to upsell whenever the opportunity presents itself!

Beanisms

Building on Success – Upselling

Upselling is a lot easier than a first-time sale

Upselling is easier and more time-efficient than cold-call selling because all the groundwork has already been laid. Existing customers are no longer prospects. They have already been qualified, their needs have been identified, and they know you and your successful track record as a training supplier. These existing customers are golden opportunities for you and your organization — so long as you make the effort to reach out for them.

Upselling is about education, not manipulation

Too many people think that upselling means selling customers additional goods or services they don't really need just to increase your profit margin. That's not upselling — it's manipulation. It has nothing to do with the consultative selling process. Real upselling is about educating the customers to ways they can leverage their initial investment to get the most out of their experience with you and your center. When you focus your efforts on educating customers about the services that will maximize their learning experience, their return on investments, and their success in achieving their goals, the add-on will practically sell itself.

Upselling, like most things in IT training sales, works best when you prepare

Be organized as you explore your customers' future needs. Prepare for logical upsales by establishing a schedule to check on your customers' future training needs and develop an action plan for selling to those needs. Know when your students will complete their current programs and be ready to talk to them about the next logical steps in their career development path or the next phase of an organization's technology strategy.

Any time can be the right time to ask for referrals from your customers

When is the best time to ask for referrals? Whenever circumstances are right for introducing your request naturally and unobtrusively into your conversations with customers or students. This could be during an initial meeting with a prospective customer, at the final meeting of a class, during a break in a workshop or lab session, while offering a promotion during a telemarketing call or during a formal business review, etc.

Your instructors spend more time than anyone else with your customers, so use them as an upselling resource

Remember that your instructors are a potent resource for upselling when you involve them in marketing your learning organization. Enlist your instructors into your sales effort by educating them about the role they can play, preparing them for their supportive marketing role, and offering support as needed.

Ongoing relationships with corporate customers are developed and maintained through upselling

Ideally, your goal with every corporate customer is to establish an ongoing partnership. This positions you to serve the needs of the company as they evolve over time. Upselling is a natural element in developing and nurturing that relationship. It allows you to link the end of one sales cycle with the beginning of another, moving smoothly from program to program, constantly discovering new opportunities and challenges.

Chapter 7

Blended Learning Solutions: There's Money in Mystery

Newsflash:

A national telecommunications firm needed to introduce 500 members of its software development team to a new networking protocol as soon as possible. The IT trainer developed a synchronous ILT solution that applied videoconferencing technology to link together learners spread over thousands of miles. The training was successfully completed in 4 days.

Newsflash:

A manufacturing firm introducing new production technology needed to provide basic operations training for line personnel. Participants were given an overview of the technology with a video and a two-hour pre-work assignment. This was followed by a self-study e-learning module that included a post-assessment. On completing these pre-requisites, the learners attended an ILT event that provided in-depth information about system technology as well as hands-on skills practice. Online links to reference materials were provided for learners to use after the workshop. These online materials allow learners to explore topics in greater depth with resources that are regularly refreshed and updated.

Newsflash:

A large international financial management firm deployed a new accounting system that would be used by each of its more than 20,000 employees around the world. To address the widely varying needs of this diverse learning audience, an IT training developer provided a customized CD-ROM pre-work self-study and practice program that participants used on their own time. Synchronous distance-learning events were then scheduled by region for blocks of learners. Online e-learning and skills practice activities were also provided for learners who were unable to attend the workshops. The training included online assessments for all training events, follow-up coaching, mentoring, and e-learning support. A threaded online discussion was developed for learners to access after the training. This follow-up feature allowed the participants to stay in touch with one another, ask questions, share insights, and post additional resources.

Newsflash:

It's not your parents' learning environment any more.

Each of these success stories demonstrates just a few of the ways in which the landscape for trainers and training has changed dramatically, especially in the world of information technology. Today, the creative application of blended learning techniques has revolutionized the way we solve specific training problems for our IT customers. Where traditional solutions might have been prohibitively expensive, time-consuming, or simply impossible, innovative hybrid learning programs were able to rise to the challenge.

Each of these groundbreaking programs was designed by training specialists who understood that a single solution could not be applied to fit every need. These curriculum designers invested time during the first and second stage of the selling process to closely examine the challenges facing their customer. They then tailored a customized learning solution that provided a laser-like focus on the learners' needs, met the customer's schedule, and didn't break the bank in the process.

So how about you? How is your organization using blended learning to enhance the training experiences of your students? Are you already a "new age" salesperson who's seen the blended future of IT learning and reached out for it? If so, good for you! Don't spend all your newfound income in one place!

But if you're still selling and designing your IT training the old-fashioned way, then let's start at the beginning....

Blended Learning: A Definition

What exactly does the term "blended learning," sometimes called hybrid or integrated learning, mean?

As you might expect, definitions vary depending on how training providers interpret the concept. While the term "blended learning" is still fairly new, the concept has been around for some time. For my purposes, an effective working definition of "blended learning" is:

- Any combination of learning methodologies, including e-learning and other resource materials, that can be combined with ILT (Instructor-Led Training) to provide the most efficient, effective, and viable solution to a client's learning problem.

The characteristic that most distinguishes blended learning from its more traditional counterparts is its flexibility. Blended learning solutions can be customized and reconfigured to provide the most viable solution to solve a learner's problem. The training designer's task is to choose from among various methods, modules, and measurements to select those that will be most effective and efficient. No single approach is valued more highly than others because solutions are selected based on a customer's particular needs and learning style.

With a blended learning solution, students can learn:

- What they want to learn (and only what they want to learn),
- When they want to learn,
- How they want to learn, and
- Within their budget and their schedule.

The many options now available to the IT training industry provide seemingly unlimited opportunities for us to design programs tailored to the specific needs, scope, and budget of all our customers. We can now provide more opportunities than ever for our learners to "get" the curriculum content we offer, to retain that knowledge, and to then apply the skills they learn effectively on the job.

Blended learning is also highly adaptable to learners' skill levels. It offers us an excellent opportunity to overcome learner anxiety about technology-based training by designing blended solutions that accommodate and build on the foundation of each student's capabilities.

For example, a blended program can introduce e-learning skills to an audience in small increments, phased in slowly over time. Initially, a short classroom session can be held to teach first-time learners the point-and-click basics of system navigation. This class sets the stage for a smooth transition into a new learning environment. By working in small steps and providing support along the way, trainers can make this change easier and less traumatic for these anxious beginners.

Finally, blended learning solutions are efficient. Corporations that invest large sums in purchasing and implementing traditional classroom learning are understandably reluctant to replace those programs and change their strategy. When we offer a blended learning option, we can give added life to existing material by adapting all or part of it into a broader design that includes e-learning and other training methods. We're able to apply a kind of bottom-line Darwinism to our program design, selecting and keeping the programs that work, and discarding whatever does not. As we gain experience with blended programs, our track record of successes and failures lets us continually hone our design choices into more efficient and effective arrangements of content, medium, and methodology.

Getting Started with Blended Learning Solutions

Designers of blended learning solutions make decisions in many directions and dimensions: What will the learning elements be? How big will they be? In what sequence will they be arranged? How long will the learner have to complete the training…or is there any deadline at all? When and how often will the learner's progress be assessed? How will successful completion of the training be defined? The answers to these and many other questions are woven together to form the canvas on which designers paint their unique training picture for each customer.

This far-reaching flexibility may seem daunting at first to trainers and salespeople whose experience is limited to more traditional learning methods. If blended learning is new to you, consider easing your way into this exciting new market opportunity by thinking of the learning process as a continuum that challenges both you and your learners to move in slow and steady steps from the known and familiar to the new and unfamiliar.

You can start by simply applying the same principles that work so effectively for you in developing your ILT curriculum. Where do you always begin? With clarifying the real objectives of your learning solution, of course! What do the learners really need to know? And why?

What will happen to them if they don't learn what they need to know? How will things change for the better when they achieve their objectives? And so forth...you know the drill! Once you've asked and answered these questions, you're already well on your way to selling a blended learning solution.

An effective strategy for starting up a blended solution is to begin by assessing an existing learning model. Ask your customer about what has worked well in the past, and what may be working well now. If you're with a current customer, for example, you can review the training you've provided previously — probably an ILT class or workshop solution. As you discuss past successes with your customer, ask yourself questions like:

- How can we build upon and extend that learning modality to achieve this customer's desired objectives?

- How can that training be modified to transfer knowledge more effectively into an individual learner's life, or into the corporation's methods and culture?

- How can we extend the effectiveness of the current classroom learning experience into other available options?

As you develop answers for these and similar questions, you will steadily and methodically make the transition from the familiar confines of classroom learning and traditional self-study to the new modalities of blended solutions.

Some advantages of building a new hybrid-learning curriculum on the foundation of an existing program include:

- *Familiarity*

  You and your learner audience have already worked with the existing program and its content. You know what it teaches, how it works, and what to expect. Most importantly, you know that it's effective. It achieves the objectives it is designed to achieve.

- *Efficiency*

  The more you're able to "piggyback" new methodologies onto an existing model, the less development work you have to do. For example, a learning path that directs a student to read a chapter of a workbook, view an existing video, or complete a module of a CBT presentation can offer a fresh learning perspective on a topic while recycling training elements that would otherwise be discarded or shelved.

- *Cost-effectiveness*

  Less development work translates directly into lower costs. Extending the life of a training program also incrementally increases the value of that material. While these factors don't automatically translate into lower costs for blended learning solutions, they do create efficiencies that can significantly offset the costs of any new IT technology incorporated into the blended solution.

Stage 1: Discovering Blended Learning Solution Opportunities

If your customers aren't familiar with blended learning solutions, chances are they will start the discussion assuming that you plan to recommend a single modality solution — a workshop, a self-study program, etc. Of course, that's what you will recommend if that option is right for the customer. If, however, you find that a blended solution is more appropriate, you'll want to explore that option more fully to see if an opportunity really exists.

When a customer indicates a need or wish for any of the following features, consider offering a blended learning solution:

Flexible Scheduling, Flexible Delivery Methods, Etc.

How many times have your customers — both individual and corporate — been frustrated by scheduling conflicts that prevent them from attending a training workshop? When someone works an evening or rotating shift schedule, it may be difficult or impossible to schedule an ILT class to accommodate that person's need. A blended solution can solve this problem by limiting or bypassing ILT sessions altogether. A learning path can be mapped that applies e-learning, online tutorials, self-paced study guides, distance learning, or other options in place of the traditional classroom experience.

Scheduled and Unscheduled Downtime

In many industries, workers regularly experience non-productive, scheduled downtime for equipment cleaning, routine maintenance, personnel shift changes, restocking, material change out, and so forth. These blocks of scheduled downtime can be made productive when workers use them to complete small self-study segments of a blended learning program. Training participants can also transform unscheduled downtime, such as a system crash, equipment breakdown, inventory shortage, cancelled meeting, etc., into valuable training time by completing small, self-paced learning segments within a larger blended program.

Key Personnel, Small-Team Training

Corporate IT managers are frequently challenged to train an entire support group or development team without reducing the group's level of productivity. The entire team can't attend a training class at one time, and small group workshops may not be financially feasible. A blended learning solution can resolve this kind of dilemma in various ways. For example, small groups can alternate training segments. Some can complete self-study or e-learning components while others attend short workshops or lab units. Perhaps a self-study e-learning program can be designed that will eliminate the need for classroom sessions altogether.

By carefully planning schedules and arranging learning objects, a client with scheduling problems can train entire teams with little or no measurable impact on performance or productivity.

Geographically Dispersed Learner Populations

Large corporations often want to train groups at the same time when they implement new procedures, technology, products, etc. If these groups are distributed across the country or the globe, gathering them together for one or more workshops can be prohibitively expensive and logistically impractical. Travel costs, time away from the job, and related expenses make it difficult to send employees to a single training site. A blended solution that offers a mix of e-learning, on-site training, and self-study supplemented with other learning tools can offer a workable alternative to this otherwise perplexing problem.

Various Learning Methods and Pathways

- *Accommodating a range of learning styles within a student population*

  Traditional ILT or classroom learning ordinarily makes no accommodation for the varieties of learning styles within a group. Blended learning solutions allow curriculum designers to correct this inherent weakness by designing different paths and using various learning objects that can be adapted to individual learners' styles. Basic patterns and pathways can be established as learning templates, but customizing variables can be added to target specific programs to learners' needs based on the insights you gather during your research phase of the selling process.

- *Accommodating variances in learner skill levels, ability, and experience*

  Virtually every experienced teacher and trainer knows the challenge of teaching groups in which learners have widely varying levels of knowledge or skill. When the session is paced for the faster learners, the material confuses or frustrates the slower

149

participants. By gearing the class for the less knowledgeable students, others can quickly become bored and lose interest in the session.

Blended learning options allow trainers to track learners at the right pace for their needs and abilities. For example, self-study reinforcement can bring less skilled learners up to a defined skill level before they attend an ILT event with their more skilled or experienced colleagues. Alternately, learners with greater ability may be given a combination of self-study and mentoring that moves them directly to a competency assessment, bypassing ILT events completely.

- *Compatibility Between Learning Topics and Learning Objects*

  Certain subjects are more effectively taught in a classroom environment where people can discuss, interact, and practice skills together with others. Programs teaching interpersonal skills, such as sales, customer service, problem-solving, team leadership, or crisis management, lend themselves readily to a classroom. Technical subjects, such as application software training, or network setup and integration, can be taught effectively within various settings. This training may include lab or e-learning components to provide the student with system-based simulation activities. This work can be designed as self-study, mentored learning, e-learning, or a classroom activity.

- *Time zone, geographical, budget, and work pattern constraints*

  As we've seen, group training can be a challenge when trainees are scattered in different locations throughout the country or the world. Blended learning solutions, including a mix of synchronous or asynchronous distance-learning options, save both time and money by eliminating travel expenses, and keeping workers close to their base of operations.

  Limited training budgets offer still more opportunities for designing and implementing blended learning solutions. If a customer tells you there isn't enough budget, you might suggest a simple blended approach: For example, a print-based program can be supplemented with CBT tutorials and online assessment tools.

This could reduce overall training costs while also successfully improving the quality of training, the quantifiable results, and the customer's ROI.

- *Tracking Results: Quantifying Student Performance with Learning Management Systems & Assessments*

  If your customers are equipped with a Learning Management System, or LMS, they have the ability to track the skills, the learning paths, and the performance of many different groups or individuals. But don't make assumptions: Just because they have this technology doesn't mean they use it effectively. You may be able to offer significant value-added support for your corporate customers by assisting in the design, development, and administration of the company's LMS tracking and reporting system. As you know, an LMS can have a significant impact on any company's training productivity and efficiency. Any assistance you are able to offer can markedly increase your mindshare with the client, giving you a decisive advantage in competitive bidding situations.

  Pre- and post-training assessment tools are valuable quantifiers that can measure learners' progress with the blended learning solution you develop. Managers can use assessments to track the progress and evaluate the ability of individual learners or groups of students. Because they provide "before and after" measurements for each learner, assessment tools can be especially helpful to reassure decision-makers who are uncertain about the blended solution option.

Effective Questioning to Discover Blended Learning Opportunities

Many of the background questions you ask to discover blended learning opportunities are similar to those used to identify more traditional options. These include questions targeted at understanding the customer's basic situation, such as:

- What is the current system infrastructure in your organization?

- How does your organization currently use IT?

- How are your employees now trained to use this technology?

- Is employee certification a goal of your training strategy?

You also ask questions aimed at defining the customer's business problem, such as:

- What are your organization's business goals? What is its overall strategy for achieving those goals?

- What compelling problem(s) are you trying to solve?

- What challenges are you facing in meeting your goals?

- Do you think you'll be able to meet your goals with your current in-house skill sets?

- What changes are you planning to make in your business?

- What role do you plan for technology in solving problems/implementing changes in your business?

And finally, you have questions to heighten the customer's awareness of how important it is that the problem be solved — and soon!

- What would happen if your mission-critical systems failed? How do you think your sales, service, and security would be compromised?

- What is the true cost of downtime in your organization?

- How is your current employee training system contributing to downtime? (Or: How does your current training contribute to lower productivity because of time away from the job?)

- What will happen if your IT system users are not trained, and stay in their current jobs?

Stage 2: Establishing the Value of the Blended Solution

Your purpose in this phase of the sale is to set the stage for offering a blended learning solution to your customer. As always, this means helping the customer measure the cost of his or her current problem, defining a specific value for that problem, and creating a "vision of success" to help the customer envision the improvements your solution will create.

You must, however, be cautious here. In a very real sense, the "product" you are offering is fundamentally different from the kind of training to which your customer is accustomed. Your success in selling a blended solution will hinge on your recognition that the pressures on your client and the client's learners are different from those that motivated them to buy ILT training in the past. Those pressures — a dispersed workforce or sharply reduced travel budgets, for example — must outweigh the anxieties that learners, managers, and risk-averse decision-makers may feel about the new and unfamiliar learning methodologies you are recommending.

If you've been successful offering similar solutions in the past, don't hesitate to tell your prospects about those successes. A testimonial from a satisfied customer, including a review of ROI figures, may be just what you need to replace anxiety with an appreciation of the many efficiencies made possible with hybrid learning options.

As we've seen, the benefits of blended solutions are numerous, and these solutions are typically customized to the specific concerns or needs of an individual or group. This is why establishing the value of a blended solution is often easier than convincing customers of the effectiveness of this training methodology. If you listened carefully to your customers and fully understand their needs, you should have plenty of information to establish and demonstrate the value of your solution in ways that are convincing and indisputable.

Once you've decided that the opportunity for a blended solution exists, you're ready to ask questions that will gather information, define the problem, and build value for your recommended solution. During this critical discovery stage, your questions will gather additional background data about the customers' situation while guiding the conversation toward the blended option. These questions may include:

- What changes are you planning to implement in your organization?
- How are you training and testing your IT system users now?
- Are you trying to fill a skills gap in your IT technology? (If yes, describe.)
- Do you have an LMS? If so, how are you currently using it?

If your customers' answers to these questions suggest a blended option, you can then focus your questions on areas that will enhance the value of that particular solution. Such questions might include:

- Are you facing time or budget constraints with this training challenge? (Or: Is the travel budget for training a concern in your organization?)
- Will you be training a diverse group of learners from different job categories?
- Where are the learners located? (One location? Dispersed in multiple locations?)
- Of your training or reference resources you're now using, what do you think works particularly well? (What doesn't work well?)
- How important will it be for you to evaluate and quantify each learner's progress?
- How would a modular learning approach that provides learning in small segments offer advantages for your learners over the way they're now organizing their training time?

As your customers respond to these questions, you will, as always, listen closely to their answers and search for clues to the needs and priorities that define their sense of value. You'll typically find that prospects who express concerns about time commitments, scheduling for ILT programs, budget issues, Just-In-Time training, and other flexibility-related issues are excellent candidates for a blended learning recommendation.

Stage 3: Offering the Blended Learning Solution

As you know, the goal of Stage 3 is to propose the right solution, and close the sale.

When you reach this point, you should have established a relationship of trust with the customer, built and established the value of a blended solution, quantified the value by calculating its ROI, and prepared yourself for the close by thinking through possible objections and how you'll respond if they come up.

Of course, there's a good chance that yours is not the only option on the table for your customer. Your competitors may be waiting in the wings with alternative proposals to present. As I've said earlier, never assume that price is the driving criterion behind the decisions our customers make when they choose between two or more training suppliers. Experience within our industry shows that our clients will usually select training vendors who offer the greater perceived expertise rather than the lowest price. You can help establish your credentials and underscore your customer's perception of your expertise by clearly understanding and explaining the benefits of blended learning, and discussing them knowledgeably.

Your next task is to emphasize the right benefits of your proposed solution to close an agreement and potentially upsell the customer.

Leveraging the Benefits of Blended Learning Solutions

When you consider the many benefits of a blended solution, you may be tempted to think of it as an embarrassment of riches! So, which do you present, describe, and leverage to convince your customer that your solution is the right way to go? Of course, that's determined by what the customer tells you is important. Generally speaking, though, the core benefits for all blended learning solutions will revolve in some way around the idea of flexible learning paths.

When those paths are administered and supported by a Learning Management System (LMS), the potential value of a blended solution can increase exponentially. The LMS can be integrated with a customized program to give the customer much more effective control over each student's curriculum and learning path. With the click of a mouse, a training manager can answer questions like:

- Where, at this moment, is any given student on his or her individualized learning path? (How much progress has he or she made? How much longer will it take him or her to complete the assigned program? Etc.)
- How well is the learner doing?
- How does the learner compare to his or her peers who've taken the same program? Etc.

An LMS makes it possible for managers to easily review their employees' learning history and their progress in developing critical work skills. This can be an especially valuable feature for those decision-makers who express concern about how their employees may use — or abuse — the freedom that self-study or self-directed programs provide.

Closing the Sale of a Blended Learning Solution

The close of the blended solution sale, like every effective close, should make it easy for the customer to say "yes." Remember the assumptive close that shuts out the "no" option by offering a choice between two "yes" alternatives. For example, a question like, "Do you want to start this program next week or two weeks from now?" tells the customer that you already assume that the decision has been made, and you're ready to get the ball rolling on implementation. Saying "no" becomes much harder for the customer. If he or she has no serious objections at that point, he or she will usually move forward with your recommendations.

Other straightforward closing requests for blended solutions can include:

- Is there anything else we can do to help you feel comfortable about presenting this recommendation for a blended solution to your manager?
- Does this solution seem like the right one to solve your problem?
- Have I answered all your questions about how this blended solution will work for you and your employees?

Handling Objections to Blended Learning Solutions

Many of the objections we hear about blended learning solutions revolve around the same issues of money and time we saw with more traditional training proposals. We discussed these objections, and some effective responses to them, in Chapter 5, "Offering the Solution." However, the unique characteristics of blended learning, together with the lack of experience many decision-makers have with these solutions, can lead to specialized concerns or objections that you should be prepared to handle. Wary training consumers who've grown accustomed to ILT solutions may be confused about the many non-classroom options they see in today's marketplace. Perhaps they're uncomfortable with what they consider an "unproven" product or method. Or maybe they're just anxious about taking a risk on something that hasn't yet been given a reassuring seal of approval by their senior management.

Whatever the immediate cause of your customers' concern, it can't be said too often that the best way for you to counter any objection is to prepare for it. As we've seen, the vast majority of the objections are predictable, and there's no excuse for you to be surprised or unprepared for most of the objections your customers raise — even to your blended learning proposals!

Examples of typical objections to blended solutions, and some recommended responses to them, include the following:

- *How do I know it will work?*

  This is perhaps the most frequently voiced objection to the blended solution, and one you must be prepared to answer. This question may arise out of simple uncertainty over an unknown or untried approach. Perhaps your customer has heard horror stories from associates or co-workers who've seen poorly designed blended programs fail spectacularly in other companies. Whatever the source of this concern, you'll have to be ready with a lot more than just the functional equivalent of "trust me, it'll be fine!" An anxious customer, especially a corporate decision-maker fearful about the implicit risk of this decision, will almost always retreat to the "no" option if you fail to offer some form of substantive assurance.

  Prepare case studies or reports outlining the experiences of your previous clients and discuss them with your hesitant customers. In fact, a case study can be an excellent tool for presenting and describing the blended solution approach even before objections arise. A description of an implementation scenario can be the "picture worth a thousand words" that helps skeptical prospects see how the blended learning option can be integrated effectively into their environment.

  You may have even better luck responding to this objection by offering a free "test drive" of a blended learning program for the customer. Offer to let the decision-maker try out a sample program, attend a class, work with e-learning components, and more to gain first-hand experience with the content and methodology you're recommending. This sample will demonstrate your confidence and pride in your product, and let your customer experience your technology-enhanced learning options first-hand. Once your customer accepts this offer, your training program takes over the job of selling — and a well-designed blended learning program always does a great job of selling itself.

- *What are your competencies? (Why do you say you can do this?)*

  This is a fundamental question about trust, and it typically comes up early in the discussion of a blended learning option. Even if you have a track record of success with the customer delivering traditional IT training, risk-averse managers will raise concerns about your abilities in this area before committing either personnel or money to your proposal.

If you have a track record of success delivering blended learning to others, share that information with your customer. Case studies, testimonials, and names and phone numbers of satisfied customers can all go a long way toward overcoming concerns about your abilities. Again, you may wish to give the customer an opportunity to try out all or portions of a blended program for some "hands-on" experience with this approach to IT training.

If you don't have extensive experience with blended solutions, consider forming partnerships with other suppliers who can deliver specialized segments of your blended solutions. By bringing multiple players together to develop specific, customer-focused solutions, you can enhance a customer's confidence by demonstrating that many resources — not just one — are working together to forge the right solution for his or her particular needs.

- *How can I be sure my employees will do the work assigned to them?*

This question typically reflects the decision-maker's own anxieties about both the new learning environment and the freedom it affords learners who will study at their own pace and on their own time. First, point out to managers who raise this objection that, whether they realize it or not, their employees are already "doing the work" of learning what they need to know, at their own pace, just to keep up with the critical demands of their jobs. A blended learning solution would provide them with a far more efficient, well-structured path for learning their job skills.

If a corporate client who raises this question has access to a Learning Management System, you can describe the various options for tracking, reporting, and testing that can be incorporated into the automated management of your program. You can also point out how the results of performance assessments completed before or after training experiences can be stored and organized on the system. Again, a case study illustrating how an LMS tracks information associated with a blended learning program can help reduce or eliminate these concerns.

- *I'd love to go ahead with this, but our CFO says there's no way we're going to spend money on this.*

  This objection has nothing to do with your proposal or the effectiveness of your blended solution. It turns out you weren't talking to the right decision-maker! Your challenge at this point is to gain access to that decision-maker and link your blended solution back to the basic business problem it is designed to solve. Make sure the decision-maker understands that your recommendation is a means to an end — a quantifiable end, represented by the ROI you defined. Link your business solution to the vision of success it is designed to achieve. Then, reinforce your proposal with the support of your internal advocate (that person who told you he or she would "love to go ahead with this"). This approach will often overcome any resistance from these "hidden decision-makers."

- *This seems like a confusing (complex) way to train people!*

  Customers familiar with single-modality training (workshops, self-study programs, etc.) may object to the seeming complexity of blended learning, especially when it includes e-learning components. As an IT sales professional, it is up to you to familiarize yourself with each relevant product and modality, and be able to describe and demonstrate each of them, if appropriate, to a customer. Point out the smooth interaction of different modalities and how they work together to create an integrated package of learning that meets the customer's needs. One effective way to overcome this objection is to offer the customer free pre-sale technical support to help overcome these anxieties.

- *I (the decision-making manager) don't believe in e-learning.*

  Such straightforward statements are a clear indicator of a corporate culture where senior management has made it clear that money will not be wasted on "newfangled" ideas like e-learning or blended solutions. The best way to succeed in making a cultural shift with such organizations is to contact senior management and win a buy-in to your offerings.

Take the time to educate your prospect about your content, method, and implementation strategy — and how all of these elements can combine to deliver a quantifiable ROI. Be sure to offer key decision-makers the opportunity to try out your e-learning. Whenever possible, let decision-makers "test drive" a program to see for themselves the value and the potential of this learning technology. Stress that with e-learning, one size definitely does not fit all, and that the very best training today is in blended programs that draw the strengths of many different modalities to enhance the learner's experience.

Winning that buy-in will not come easily. Along with your standard features and benefits presentation, you may wish to provide an internal demonstration for managers and prospective trainees. Offer training in how to successfully roll out a hybrid learning solution, and oversee the deployment of a solution to ensure its success. Experience has shown many in our business that if you don't take the time to educate your customers on how to properly roll out a blended learning solution, chances are good that they will fail. That failure will only reinforce any prejudices they may have against the solutions you're promoting — and that, of course, is the opposite of what you're trying to achieve!

- *We have a corporate firewall. We can't use any training that has an external e-learning component.*

The CIO or corporate IT staff may tell you that their rigid network security makes e-learning unworkable for their company. You may be told, for example, that internal security procedures make it impossible for employees to access the corporate network from their homes or other remote locations.

This objection typically arises when the salesperson hasn't done an effective job helping the company's CIO or IS group understand the true value of resolving these firewall issues. Remember that most IS departments go out of their way to prevent any breaches of their corporate system security. They have a natural and almost instinctive aversion to anything

161

perceived as a potential compromise to their security. However, if you take the time with the decision-maker to explain the value of the learning solution you recommend, you will find there are ways around this problem.

Here again, your task is to educate the client. You might explain, for example, that a blended solution could be developed and implemented inside the company's firewall. You could develop a curriculum that schedules participants for a daily one-hour e-based training program that they complete as they would a self-study course or ILT workshop. When this plan is implemented, be sure to communicate the ROI for your solution by tracking and reporting the increased productivity that results from the training.

- *We bought a million dollar e-learning library a few years ago and everybody hated it. Nobody used it! So please, don't talk to me about anything like e-learning — we've learned our lesson.*

This challenging objection is an invitation for you to demonstrate the kind of professional consultative skills that can lead to a long-term partnership with a customer. Your client has told you that something involving e-learning went seriously wrong in the past. You must find out what that was, explain how the problem occurred, and then demonstrate how you can ensure the effectiveness of your prospective solution.

Ask questions to help you assess where the disconnect occurred between the customer's original problem and the solution he or she attempted to impose upon it. Your questions may include:

- What business goal were you trying to achieve (or: what business problem were you trying to solve) when you spent that much on an e-solution?

- What program did you purchase? (Obtain a general description of the program, including its objectives and methods.)

- What kind of preparation were your employees given before the program was implemented?

- What learning environment was provided for learners?

- What kind of technical support was available for the e-learners when they ran into trouble with the training?

- What reward or recognition did the learner receive upon successful completion of the training?

Chances are good that after you ask a series of questions like these, you'll have a clear picture of one or more possible problem areas in your prospect's original e-learning implementation strategy. With your evaluation at hand, your response to the customer might be framed as a comment similar to this one:

"We had a client recently who had a similar experience. We helped him understand that you can't just purchase something as complex and sophisticated as an e-learning library, and expect your employees to pick it up and automatically develop new skills. That just doesn't work.

"We mapped out the contents of our library and linked them directly to the specific problems the employees were experiencing. We created a customized learning path for each employee, and gave everyone an orientation to the program so they knew which course to take, when to take it, and how they would apply what they learned on the job. We built in assessment checkpoints so the learners and their managers could check their progress at every step along the way. We also tracked their progress in the company's LMS. When the employees completed their programs, their success was recognized with course-completion certificates that now hang near their workstations.

"And we got results! After we implemented our solution, employee access to the online library increased by 75%, the employee knowledge base increased by 30% and productivity increased by 25%. And on top of that, the participants felt they got so much out of their learning experiences that we got many requests for new programs to be added this year."

One final objection to blended solutions is based on the fundamental misunderstanding that blended solutions should automatically cost less than ILT solutions. This myth was born about the time blended solutions were first introduced. Many salespeople and customers assumed that blended learning should be less costly because it often eliminated the need for classrooms, instructors, travel costs, and other expenses associated with traditional ILT.

While cost-efficiencies are indeed a part of the equation, they are not the only part. The high-tech components of most blended learning solutions usually add costs that may offset any realized savings. While it is certainly possible that a blended solution may reduce the total cost of training for a customer, it is equally possible that high-tech support for multiple learning objects could actually increase overall costs.

As IT training sales professionals, we must clearly communicate the truth about the pricing of blended learning — namely, that there's no fixed rule about whether it will cost more or less than other options. Our task is to focus on meeting the customer's needs and fulfilling our ROI commitment rather than emphasizing one-to-one price comparisons.

A final word about preparing for objections: You know they are inevitable, and you know you should prepare for them. One way to be ready for future objections to blended solutions is to build a personalized database of the objections you hear, and include your effective responses to them. By tracking this information, even a sale you lose can become a helpful resource in the future. Your case studies offer insight into real customer concerns that could become stumbling blocks to a sale — and they give you the chance to prepare a more persuasive response to an objection the next time it comes up. Believe it or not, I've found that sometimes talking about what doesn't work can be an extremely powerful sales strategy. Customers are often very appreciative and responsive when I openly describe some of the challenges they may face, and acknowledge the fact that e-learning is not a panacea that can cure all ills.

Stage 4: Upselling the Blended Learning Solution

As with every learning option, blended learning solutions offer many opportunities to lay the groundwork for future blended learning sales, and to ask for referrals. As you become more familiar with blended learning and its sophisticated options, you will see many opportunities for upselling. Some of the options you offer as value-added benefits for some customers may be transformed into upselling opportunities for others. LMS administration, resource planning, front- and back-end analysis, vendor management, competency testing, certification testing, and much more are all options that could be upsold and added to a blended learning package.

Offering Blended Learning Solution Add-Ons

When presenting and closing on a blended learning sale, think through all the beneficial add-ons that might be appropriate for your customer. These might include:

- *Complementary programs or classes*

  When appropriate, offer selected learners the opportunity to attend a special event or class that is relevant to their current program of instruction. Offers of "free" learning opportunities build good will and loyalty, particularly among your more motivated learners. They also expose your students to other program topics, technologies, or learning methods that can stimulate thinking about future buying decisions. You may also wish to consider offering programs to assist corporate clients, such as coaching or workshops on change management or other relevant issues.

- *Certification programs*

  If you see that a learner's current blended learning program can be efficiently mapped to a certification process, consider upselling the certification component to increase the program's value. Certification testing can be a particularly useful add-on benefit for customers with clearly defined career objectives, and it strengthens the reward value of the learning in the eyes of your students.

- *Virtual labs*

  After outlining a proposed learning path for a customer, you can build value for blended learning prospects by offering "free" online interactive experiences to supplement the learner's program of instruction. Learners can use these lab opportunities to practice the skills they learn, on their own time and as often as they wish. Learners anxious about trying e-learning for the first time will value the chance to learn navigation skills and other basics in self-paced lab sessions separate from their normal learning path.

- *LMS support services*

    When you discover early in the selling process that your corporate customer expects to integrate an LMS with your blended solution, you can expect your customer to ask, "How will your products and content interact with my LMS, or the LMS I am buying?" Once you answer that question, you are in a position to offer add-on support services to really build your value and your partnership with your corporate customer.

    Assistance with LMS administration is probably the greatest add-on value that customers can obtain from their suppliers. You gain a significant advantage with your clients when you're able to offer services that support the administration and resource planning of a corporation's Learning Management System. This can include front- and back-end analysis, competency assessment, individual or group performance reporting, integrating new programs into an existing system, and much more. Be sure to think through your own resources and the costs of offering this support before discussing this service with your corporate customers.

- *Assessment management*

    The most common concerns raised about blended learning — effectiveness, learner accountability, and vendor competency — can often be answered with assessment tools that tabulate and track each learner's success. Assessments can be the "proof in the pudding" at every stage in the blended learning process. Among the assessment tools you can offer your customers are:

    Learning style assessment to determine how each student learns best, and help the customer make better decisions about which learning paths each student should follow.

    Pre-learning assessments can identify each learner's skill level to ensure that the training challenge is properly adapted to his or her abilities. By identifying and measuring the skills gap of each learner, curriculum designers can prescribe customized learning paths for each individual. This customization improves overall learning efficiency by tracking learners to programs that are right for their skill levels. Advanced students aren't bored taking basic prerequisite course materials, and beginners are not overwhelmed or frustrated by unfamiliar material they don't understand.

Checkpoint assessments measure the learner's progress at milestones along the learning path. These brief reviews:

- Track the pace of learning (Is the learner on schedule?),

- Evaluate the learner's comprehension of specific learning topics (Did the learner understand and master this topic?), and

- Measure the learner's progress against anticipated growth (Has the learner achieved the skill level expected at this point along the learning path?).

Post-learning assessments, the "final tests" of blended learning solutions, tell students, administrators, and employers whether a student has achieved the goals of the training. By comparing these results with pre-learning assessments, managers and trainers can decide if the training succeeded, and can develop a solid ROI calculation to quantify the value of a blended training solution.

Asking for Referrals

When a customer is pleased with you and your solutions, he or she is often happy to share the benefits you've offered with his or her friends and associates. As always, don't passively wait for suggestions — be proactive, and ask for potential leads that could result in added business for you and your company. When requesting blended learning referrals, consider:

- Ask your customer contact if he or she knows of any individuals or departments within his or her organization that might benefit from blended learning solutions similar to those you've implemented successfully.

- Ask for external referrals — friends, business associates, client contacts, etc. — who may have needs for IT training, especially blended learning.

- Always ask for permission to use the customer's name when you contact the referrals, as a point of contact and familiarity.

- It is often much easier to offer e-learning demonstrations to potential referrals than to provide a classroom demonstration. With e-learning, you can simply provide an e-demo key to a potential referral. There's no need to arrange schedules for the referral to show up at a fixed time in a particular classroom on a certain date.

If you believe (as you should) that upselling is the easiest way to sell, then you should take advantage of the many upselling options and opportunities opened up to you by blended learning. So, how are you handling this aspect of your business now? Are you going back to your individual and corporate customers and offering value-added opportunities in a hybrid learning environment to gain maximum benefits from them? Are you taking advantage of the power of e-updates to your past ILT customers to advise them of new e-learning opportunities appropriate to their learning tracks? If you aren't pursuing these and other opportunities now, there's really only one question left to ask:

Why not?

Beanisms

Blended Learning Solutions — There's Money in Mystery

New technology and market pressures are fueling demand for blended learning

Advances in presentation and information technology have provided trainers with an astonishing array of options for customizing the training they provide. Content, methodology, schedule, and cost can all be adjusted to meet the needs and requirements of customers. Other pressures — tighter training budgets, more restricted travel, and greater scheduling challenges — are adding to the training market's increasingly loud clamor for blended learning options. Are you listening?

169

Do whatever you can to never say "no" to your customer's needs

There will be times when you won't be able to manage your customer's expectations. Before you simply say "no," explore every possible blended learning alternative that will let you meet all or part of your customer's request.

Remember that whenever you say "no," a salesperson from one of your competitors will be ready, willing, and able to say "yes." You never want to invite your competition in! Once they get started providing selected services for your customer, you may wake up one day to discover that your entire account has slipped away.

Blended learning technology makes "mass customization" possible

"Mass customization" seems like a contradiction in terms, and until the advent of blended learning technology, it was. The term can be defined as providing customized learning solutions for multiple learners built around a finite number of tools and skills sets.

IT curriculum designers now have the flexibility to provide multiple learners with customized learning solutions. The challenge for educators and designers is to provide a unique solution without breaking the bank. Mass customization now makes this possible by using a variety of modalities to create rich and extremely valuable learning experiences.

When building blended learning, start with existing learning modalities

One of the most effective strategies for building blended learning is to assess an existing learning model, and think through how it can be adapted or extended to achieve the learner's objectives. When you know that an existing learning object can do the job for you, don't discard it and "reinvent the wheel." Instead, modify it to more effectively transfer knowledge. Among the advantages of building your blended solutions on a foundation of existing learning objects are: Learner familiarity, efficiency, and cost-effectiveness.

A Learning Management System (LMS) makes blended learning easier to administer, support — and sell

When flexible learning paths are administered and supported by a Learning Management System (LMS), your customer will have much greater control over individual or group learning paths, the learning process, and the tracking of results. With the click of a mouse, a manager can find answers to questions like:

- Where are the learners on their learning paths? (How much progress have they made? How much longer will it take them to complete the assigned program? Etc.)

- How well are the learners doing? Are they achieving their objectives?

- How do individual learners compare with their peers now taking the same program? How are they doing in comparison to learners who took the same learning path in the past? Etc.

- What kind of ROI are we currently realizing from our training investment? Do our actual results match up favorably with our original projections?

Many objections to blended solutions are predictable, so be ready for them

Objections to blended learning revolve around the same money and time issues you encounter with more traditional solutions. However, the unique characteristics of blended learning create some new and specialized issues for which you should be prepared.

Some common objections to blended solutions include:

* How do I know it will work?

* How can I be sure my employees will do the work?

* We're not going to spend money on this.

* Our employees would just waste time if they were allowed to learn on their own.

* Blended learning is too confusing (too complex).

* We've been successful with the ILT we have, so we don't see any reason to try blended learning.

* I don't believe in e-learning.

* We can't use a blended solution with e-learning because of our corporate firewall.

* We bought an expensive e-learning library a few years ago and nobody used it.

Remember that sometimes when you candidly describe situations in which e-learning did not work effectively, you make the most powerful argument for selling this technology.

Build a library of blended learning solutions to offer as examples and demonstrations

Every blended learning proposal you present and sale you make provides you with something new for your case study library. Each program you sell can help you explain and demonstrate how this approach is applied to prospects for whom blended learning is a new concept. Your case studies can also help introduce this approach to other departments within a corporation where you have already established a professional relationship.

Chapter

Conclusion: Where Do We Go From Here?

I knew the meeting with the board would be rough. Our largest corporate client was unhappy — very unhappy. We're talking about the kind of unhappiness that brought attorneys into the room. I'd already been told that this meeting would be our last hope for salvaging this account as well as our reputation with the client. At the time, I had only been on the job for three weeks, but since I was now the Executive Vice President of Sales, it fell to me to walk into that hotel ballroom for the meeting with the client and the client's attorneys. I was responsible for coming up with a solution to a very bad situation. Oh, did I mention that the client was not happy?

As I walked into the ballroom, a grim-faced gathering stared at me silently from their seats around the conference table. The crystal chandelier shimmering above the table in the center of the room only added to the Star Chamber atmosphere. The key decision-maker for the client sat silently in his leather chair, staring straight ahead, wallowing in self-pity and righteous indignation. He said nothing, working extra hard to avoid making eye contact with me.

He let his attorney do all the talking. And talk he did. I sat there uncomfortably as he launched into an extended litany of the client's service complaints. These festering grievances had been discussed again and again between my company and the client in the months before I'd come on board, and were now sadly familiar to everyone. The client's attorney was eloquent, flamboyant, and impressive as he made his case, but his core message was simple and straightforward — "Fix these problems, or else!"

It was now my turn to speak. This client was in no mood for defensiveness and excuse-making. It was time, I realized, for something new, something bold. It was time for something that had been missing in our earlier relationship with this customer — candid honesty.

I didn't deny any of the service problems they cited. I made no excuses and I offered no apology. Instead, I laid out the simple facts, saying, "Ladies and gentlemen, we have a problem. I know we haven't met our commitments to you, and you have every right to be unhappy. But you know what? I'm going to solve this problem, and to do that, we need to have a candid conversation about what's broken here, where we're causing you the most pain, and prioritize what's got to be fixed. Then, you need to let me go away and get the job done." I paused, and pointed to the chandelier above our heads.

"But I make this promise to you…. If I don't fix these service issues by the next time I come and stand before this board, each of you will have the personal right to hang me from that chandelier. And what's more, I'll resign from my position, because I will have failed to do my job."

I went on to explain that I wasn't certain I could solve all of the complicated issues associated with this account — but if I couldn't, I'd be sure to personally explain why to them at every step of the way. And if it turned out that I didn't have what to took to set the situation right and they decided to bring someone else in to handle it, I told them I'd personally lead the charge to find that person.

They didn't need to look for anyone else. This sullen group was so disarmed by my open admission of our failures and my willingness to take responsibility for fixing the problem that they gave me the chance I was asking for. As I began investigating the complex issues surrounding this account, I discovered that our most damaging failures had been in a service area that was outside our core competencies. I was able to efficiently rectify those problems by brokering that part of the account to another vendor. By taking this approach, we were able to solve the customer's problems, save the client money, and leverage our internal resources more effectively. This client, who had been ready to both fire and sue us, was so pleased with our turnaround in service quality and responsiveness that it went on to offer us expanded training and certification opportunities in subsequent months and years. Oh, yes — I'm happy to report that I escaped the hangman's noose.

This isn't your typical sales success story, of course. It was difficult, and in many ways embarrassing, for me to face those angry stakeholders and acknowledge the many ways our company had let them down. That meeting was more of a rescue mission than a sales call. So why, then, do I look back on that experience as one of the most satisfying and pivotal events in my sales career? It certainly wasn't because I saw it as evidence of my powers of persuasion. Nor did I think of it as a demonstration of my ability to turn lemons into lemonade. Instead, it stands out in my memory because it spoke to me of the importance of both personal and professional integrity, so necessary for salespeople in their relationships with customers.

Viewed through the lens of our selling model, we see how the issue of integrity permeated every aspect of our relationship with the customer. My customer's business problem was very easy to define and understand. It had been caused by my company's failure to keep its promises. It was also painfully obvious what would happen if that problem continued, and why it was important to solve it. We were all well aware of the costs of the problem, both to the customer's budget and to my company's reputation. I also knew that the solution I offered would succeed only if it were offered in the context of candid openness and honesty, without masks, without manipulation, and without excuses. As this relationship slowly healed, the customer saw that there were meaningful actions behind my words. As trust grew once again from the positive results of those actions, growth opportunities presented themselves. Our relationship was healthy and flourishing once again.

In my experience, I've found that my customers always appreciate it when I take the bold step of actually leveling with them. When we work together to candidly address the issues facing us, the all-too-human tendency to drift into blame and recrimination evaporates in the challenge of solving a shared problem. More often than not, this approach not only enhances confidence and trust, but also turns dissatisfaction into delight as the customers see steady progress being made. They feel better and better as their list of problems gets smaller and smaller. Having weathered the crisis together, you may discover that the bonds between you and your customers become stronger than ever. Your relationship has evolved from a utilitarian customer-supplier affiliation into a partnership founded on respect and integrity. The rest, of course, is up to you.

Developing Your Personal Plan

Attitude. Integrity. Self-awareness. Empathy. Communication skills. The ability to think on your feet. These natural gifts are just some of the vital strands that are woven together into the fabric of every successful salesperson's career. If you possess these attributes, great. But as we saw early on, raw talent and natural gifts alone are not enough to guarantee success. In truth, there's nothing that can ever really guarantee your success — but there are many things you can do to put the odds in your favor.

Perhaps the best way to focus your effort to succeed is by developing a strategic plan for achieving that success.

If you've been selling for a while, then the idea of planning isn't new to you. Consider, for example, some of the areas where we've discussed planning in this book as a part of our sales process. We discussed:

- Planning for sales calls by first educating yourself about the client, and defining your short-term goals and strategies for every call.

- The process of planning and developing the right solution for your customers by first analyzing their situation, evaluating your products and services, and then recommending a specific "fit" designed specifically for each customer.

- Planning for predictable price resistance and other objections from customers and preparing effective responses to address the customers' concerns.

- Planning corporate proposals by preparing templates and other "mass customization" tools to give you a head start on addressing your customers' needs.

- Preparing "action plans" to follow up on upselling opportunities that arise with individual and corporate customers. This includes developing a schedule for contacting and following up with customers and key corporate decision-makers.

While these and many of the ideas we've discussed have been proven effective by many salespeople who work in the challenging world of IT training, you may well be asking, "Will they really be valuable for me, and are they worth the time and effort?"

Well, I've talked a lot about the idea of value in this book. Just as the real meaning of value varies from customer to customer, the real worth of the ideas I've shared in this book will vary depending on how you interpret and apply them with your customers in your specific market. One thing, however, is certain. These ideas will be nothing more than ink on paper if you do not personally take the step of transforming them into a personal and practical plan of action.

Chances are, you've been thinking about how the ideas in this book relate to you and your situation as you've been reading along — and that's good! But ideas that are not assimilated, transformed, and applied into a plan of action are like morning mists that fade with the first sunlight. If you've gained anything of value from what you've read (and I certainly hope you have), then the time has come for you to make the connection between knowledge and practice, between idea and plan.

Your life and business are both unique, so your strategy for building your business will also be unique. As you move from learning to assimilating, and then to practicing and implementing the principles outlined in this book and in the MoneyMaker 2 training program, you will find your journey a lot less confusing and challenging if you map out your route ahead of time. Don't worry — no one will hold you rigidly to your plan. If you're like most professional salespeople in this dynamic market, you'll be making many mid-course corrections along the way. And that's great! As you gain experience and new knowledge, you'll have many fresh opportunities to sharpen your focus. But you must start somewhere.

Whatever goals you may wish to attain with your personal plan, the most important thing here is to take action — to do something. The very best ideas in the world are worthless if they are never transformed into action.

Finally, I hope that this book has given you not only some ideas about how you can improve your sales performance, but also some perspective on the importance of your role in sustaining the effectiveness and integrity of the IT training industry. The strategies and lessons I've shared are yours to use and apply as you see fit. I hope they are as effective and profitable for you as they've been for me and the sales teams I've managed over the years.

I've "bean there and done that." Now it's your turn. Success and prosperity in this business can certainly be yours, but only if you choose to reach for them. That is your decision to make, and your goal to achieve.

If I were my father, this would be where I'd remind you that there's no such word as "can't." But I'm not my father, so let me say it more simply:

You can.

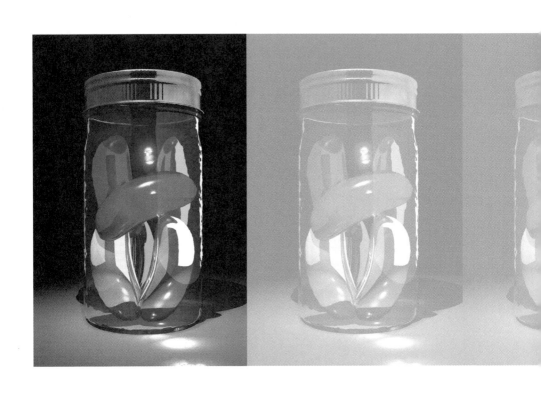

Glossary

Asynchronous Learning   Also called Location-Independent Learning. Provides delivery of interactive instruction to learners at different times and in different places. This "time-free, place-free" learning method is typically delivered via the Web or CD-ROM. It provides learners with access to resources without having to meet at the same place at the same time.

Benchmarking   Measuring against an established standard. For example, one training organization can benchmark itself against competitors by performing an item-by-item comparison of services, curriculum, pricing, etc.

Blended Learning   Any combination of learning methodologies, including e-learning and other resource materials, that can be combined with ILT (Instructor-Led Training) to provide an efficient, effective, and viable solution to a learning problem. This multimedia mix can include digital audio and video, Web-based training, performance support tools, interactive television, CD-ROMs, DVDs, teletraining, virtual labs, self-paced asynchronous e-learning, live virtual synchronous e-learning, and more.

Certification   Programs offered primarily by hardware and software vendors to recognize the knowledge and skills of support professionals and developers. The formal validation and verification that the technical skills of an individual meet the objectively defined standards established by an authoritative and recognized body.

Channel Selling   Process for selling training in which a program owner or vendor develops program materials, and sells and delivers the training through certified or authorized third parties who must meet certain quality standards to obtain the brand. (Example: Microsoft CTECS — Certified Technical Education Centers.)

Co-opetition   Competitors within an industry working together for the greater good of the total industry. Such interactions commonly take place at conventions, trade shows, conferences, etc.

E-learning   Electronic learning. Any computer-based educational methodology such as interactive CD-ROM learning, Web-based training, synchronous and asynchronous e-learning, and more.

E-LT   Virtual or Electronic Instructor-Led Training. Non-traditional learning in which a teacher leads a learning experience using Internet technology to lecture, show examples, or hold group and individual activities to communicate the curriculum from a distant location. Also sometimes referred to as Distance Learning.

Escalation Path   Technique for building and retaining trust with customers after a sale is closed and the account is passed on to operations personnel. At closing, the salesperson offers to serve as a "problem solver" acting as a liaison constantly available to handle any problems that arise with the account. Building an Escalation Path provides reassurance for the customer, helps assure his or her loyalty, and builds long-term relationships.

Gap Analysis   Technique for assessing customer need. The salesperson uses objective criteria to determine the customer's current status, and define the customer's desired status. The customer and salesperson then examine the "gap" between these two points to identify specific needs. Also referred to as Assessment Analysis.

Hard Skills Training   Usually referring to computer-based or IT training, such as Microsoft Access, Microsoft Project, A+, SQL, or related skills. Sometimes also referred to as tangible skills. Hard skills training, when combined with soft skills training, can be an effective selling tool. For example; selling a blended solution of Microsoft Project hard skills and Project Management soft skills training to promote "Using Project to Effectively Manage Engineering Projects."

Horizontal Markets Markets that define specific activities that cut across industry lines. Accountants, software developers, graphic designers, self-employed contractors, and consultants are all examples of horizontal markets. (Horizontal markets make up about 70% of IT usage in the U.S.)

ILT Instructor-Led Training. Traditional classroom learning in which a teacher leads a class or workshop using lecture, group, and individual activities to communicate the curriculum.

IT Information Technology, a term that describes all forms of technology used to create, store, exchange, and use information in different forms (data, voice, still images, video, etc.) It's a convenient term that can include both communication and computer technology.

Learning Management System (LMS) Automated system for administering the learning process within an organization. An LMS may perform a variety of functions, including tracking learner progress through programs, receiving and providing e-learning content, administering self-study programs, providing and automatically grading tests and quizzes, calculating and tracking ROI in training, etc.

Learning Object Any small instructional component that can be constructed in any format (print, audio, video, computer- or Web-based, etc.) and used a number of times and in a variety of instructional contexts. "Reusable chunks" of learning that can be re-arranged as needed to address the learner's particular needs.

Learning Tracks A grouping of related workshops or programs with a common, typically broad, focus. Typical learning tracks in IT training include job roles such as network administration, etc.

Mass Customization A technique for providing multiple learners with customized training solutions built around a finite number of tools and skill sets. Basic component templates are constructed and then customized to meet the specific needs of a client.

Mindshare Level of a vendor's presence in a customer's thoughts when confronting a need to be met or a problem to be solved. If you are the supplier of choice for IT training that a customer routinely calls because he or she respects your knowledge and understanding of the subject matter, you have dominant mindshare with that customer.

Platform   The underlying computer system on which application programs can run. On personal computers, Windows 2000 and the Macintosh are each examples of a platform.

Soft Skills Training   Usually referring to non-computer based training, such as presentation skills, time management, supervisory management, diversity, project management, or related skills. Sometimes also referred to as non-tangible skills. Soft skills training, when combined with hard skills training, can be an effective selling tool. For example, selling a blended solution of Microsoft PowerPoint hard skills and Sales Presentations soft skills training to promote "Using PowerPoint in Effective Sales Presentations."

Synchronous Learning   E-learning curriculum provided over a network or the Internet in real (synchronous) time. Chat rooms, distance learning classrooms, live audio, and interactive question and answer sessions between educators and students are all examples of synchronous learning.

Target Markets   Market segment identified by a salesperson or sales group for special attention, typically based on a defined affinity between the vendor's skills and the customers' needs.

Trial Close   Preliminary agreement obtained between a salesperson and a customer to establish commonality on a specific point.

Uncapped Accelerators   Bonus plans for salespeople that place no upper limit on bonuses that successful salespeople can achieve. The more they are able to sell, the more they earn.

Unique Competitive Advantage   The strengths of a training organization that set it apart from its competitors. This advantage may be a unique training service or methodology, speed or flexibility of service, financing options, career consultation, etc. It is best expressed in terms of specific customer benefits, not features.

Vendor-Neutral Certification   Also called cross-industry certification. A validation of a user's technical skills tied to a system function and not to a particular hardware or software manufacturer's proprietary solution. A+ and Network+ are examples of vendor-neutral certifications.

Vertical Markets   Markets organized along industry lines — that is, by the type of business or activity they do. Banking, insurance companies, and the auto industry are all examples of vertical markets.